LEARNING THROUGH SMALL GROUP DISCUSSION

A study of seminar work in higher education

Jean Rud

Society for Research into Higher Education Ltd.,
at the University of Surrey, Guildford, Surrey, GU2 5XH

Research into Higher Education Monographs

Society for Research into Higher Education, University
of Surrey, Guildford, Surrey, GU2 5XH

First published 1978, reprinted 1979

ISBN 0 900868 63 5

Printed by Direct Design (Bournemouth) Ltd., Butts Pond
Industrial Estate, Sturminster Newton, Dorset, DT10 1AZ

CONTENTS

ACKNOWLEDGEMENTS

I am grateful to the following people

for permission to refer to or quote from seminars or interviews in which they
were involved;
for permission to reproduce or refer to course outlines, contracts, reports of
experimental courses or meetings, and internal unpublished discussion
papers which they wrote;
for permission to reproduce articles or sections of articles which they wrote and
which are already in print:

Jane Beckett, John Broadbent, Alan Hobbs, Sidney Kettle, Holger Klein, Franz
Kuna, James McFarlane, Michael Parkinson, Richard Sheppard and Malcolm Seddon
at the University of East Anglia;

David Bridges, Peter Scrimshaw and their colleagues at Homerton College,
Cambridge;

Peter Chambers at Bradford College;

Gerald Collier (formerly at Bede College, Durham), and his colleagues;

Tony Hassan at Bulmershe College of Higher Education, Reading;

Stanley Nisbet at the University of Glasgow.

Thanks also to colleagues in various audio-visual centres who made it possible to
record small groups at work, especially Malcolm Freegard and the staff of the
Audio Visual Centre at the University of East Anglia.

And thanks to all the unnamed students whose discussions in seminars and
comments on seminars helped me to develop an understanding of the problems
and possibilities of small group work.

Note

All names of students and staff, where they appear in passages of transcription,
have been anonymised.

All interviews and interview/discussions were conducted by the author unless
otherwise stated.

THE AUTHOR

Jean Rudduck is a lecturer at the Centre for Applied Research in Education at the University of East Anglia, where she has directed two projects on small group work in higher education, one supported by the University Grants Committee and one by the Nuffield Foundation. Before that she worked on the Schools Council/Nuffield Foundation Humanities Curriculum Project, which was concerned with the development of discussion-based enquiry into controversial social issues in secondary schools.

Her other books are:

Dissemination of Innovation: The Humanities Curriculum Project (1976)
    Schools Council Working Paper 56   Evans/Methuen Educational
The Dissemination of Curriculum Development (with Peter Kelly) (1976)
    A European Trend Report on Educational Research   National Foundation for Educational Research Publishing Company

She has also written one booklet, and edited another, on aspects of small group work:

Teaching Symmetry Theory in Seminars: a study of innovation (1976)
    Centre for Applied Research in Education
Small Group Work in University Science Teaching: Introductory Papers (Ed.)
    (1976) Centre for Applied Research in Education

FOREWORD

Small group work, unlike the lecture, does not imply a presentation of material which is pre-planned. It demands instead a capacity to respond to developing situations in such a way as to maximise opportunities for learning. In this it may be likened to chess. It has its classic strategies, but substantial improvement of performance depends upon the analysis of one's own play and that of others. This book addresses itself to those who for a variety of reasons think that participatory small group work is or may be an appropriate medium through which to pursue their educational intentions. The aim is to help them explore both the potential and the problems of this form of teaching.

The issues and the evidence presented in this book are derived from a study of small groups at work — that is, engaged in the task of learning. The members of the small groups were university and college staff and students and the small group sessions took place as a normal part of their course. (See *Small Group Teaching Project*)

The small group sessions were recorded (with the agreement of their members) on video-tape. The recorded sessions covered a range of subject areas but there was no intention of gathering enough samples of work in each subject area to explore the hypothesis that there are differences in small group work that systematically reflect the content and mode of enquiry of different disciplines or fields of study. What emerges instead is a more general discussion of basic issues, the kind of discussion that might be helpful to the inexperienced teacher, as well as to the experienced teacher who has not before been involved in small group work — or who has been involved, has perhaps found the experience difficult, but has retained some curiosity about the nature of the problems encountered.

There are no short cuts to the improvement of one's performance in small group work, but it is possible that the observations presented here will at least provide a framework for the study of one's own sessions. The documentary evidence* (the extracts from interviews and written statements, and transcripts of discussion) may persuade the reader that an investment of time and thought would be worthwhile in terms of the seriousness of the issues that underlie the problems and the achievements of small group work.

---

*'To call something evidence is not to imply that it carries authority but merely that it is relevant to the matter under discussion.' (Humanities Curriculum Project, 1970, p. 13) The extracts from interviews etc. are not intended to suggest that this is how all students or all seminar leaders view or talk about small group work. The quotations simply suggest that this is how some students and some seminar leaders think and feel. One way of using the evidence would be to present it to students in one's seminar group as a way of opening up a discussion: do *they* feel the same way? do *they* have the same problems?

That I use 'she' when I refer to the seminar leader will not need to be excused by women readers who will recognise that this is where I identify. I am sure that men readers will be able to delete the 's' with as little resentment as I have felt in adding it in books I read.

INTRODUCTION   FOCUS AND BIAS

'Small group work' can mean many things. At one level a distinction can be made between groups which meet to learn and groups which meet to make decisions in order to take action. The committee is the most common example of the decision-making group. Groups which meet to learn may want to learn about themselves, probably by studying behaviour as it happens in the group. In this category would fall therapy groups. But groups may want to learn about matters that are specified by a curriculum, as in a school, college and university. It is the latter form of small group work, the academic learning group, that will be the focus of this book.

'Academically oriented small groups which meet to learn': the definition is still not sharp enough to provide an unambiguous point of contact between the writer and the readers of a book on small group work. In the studies that preceded the writing of this book, I decided to concentrate on one particular approach to small group work (which I call 'the seminar' even though I know that in other institutions the same approach is called 'the tutorial'). It is an approach which is widely used, an approach which has enormous potential for the development of independent and sensitive thinking in students – and yet it is, I find, an approach which it is difficult to use effectively and where, therefore, the distinctive potential for student learning is not always fully realised.

The characteristics of the 'seminar' approach are these:

—   A group of at least four students and not more than sixteen.

—   The presence of one or two staff members* (the 'seminar leaders').

—   The expectation that discussion rather than instruction will be the main mode of learning.

—   The expectation that learning will be related to student participation.

The book takes problems as a legitimate starting point, inviting the reader to accept the task of trying to understand the problems of small group work as they are documented here, and to use this understanding as the basis for studying her own small group work.

A comprehensive set of teaching tips is not on offer: teaching tips that are widely

---

*Because interest is growing in group work where the staff member is not continuously present but where she may be available for coordination and consultation, I have, in Chapter VI explored the issues that seem to be relevant to 'leaderless' group work.

applicable must be formulated at such a high level of generality that they will offer little fresh insight. And it is not really feasible to try to present *models* of successful seminars: recipes would be required, and recipes assume some standardisation of ingredients, equipment and measuring instruments. Given the diversity of our educational institutions (their traditions, their values, their personnel, their rooms, their resources and their schedules) replication of situation and circumstance is highly unlikely. Recipes would not work. Moreover, recipes would assume that one could confidently diagnose the attributes of a successful seminar, the prior assumption being that people will agree about what constitutes success!

Indeed a cavalcade of images of successful seminars could be demoralising for the teacher or lecturer who is only just managing to tread water in her small group sessions. They could make her feel that she is an isolated failure rather than one of a large company of people who are excited by the potential of small group work but find the practice difficult and are uncertain how to make things better.

So, this book presents problems, identifies issues, and offers the data of interview transcripts and discussion transcripts to give additional perspectives and richer meanings.

There could of course be bias in the selection of problems. As far as possible, the problems discussed in the pages that follow are ones that colleagues in colleges and universities — and often in the sixth forms of schools — have identified as being significant for *them*. There may also be bias in the tendency to see 'authority' as the key perspective for understanding problems in small group work. Certainly there is a preoccupation with issues of authority: the authority of the seminar leader, the authority of the institution, and the authority of knowledge. But authority is not the only major source of difficulty: this book is premised on the idea that difficulties in making the most of small group work are also related to a general inexperience of this form of learning, and concomitant uncertainties about aims and procedures, responsibilities and rights, sanctions and rewards.

Finally, readers may think it a bias to see, as I do, small group work as essentially a formal rather than an informal activity.

CHAPTER I   HARNESSING THE DISTINCTIVE POTENTIAL OF SMALL
             GROUP WORK

THE ISSUES

The lecture, traditionally, implies a one-way communication system. Lectures
may invite participation through such devices as questioning or short, localised
buzz-group discussions, but sustained interaction involving a reasonable proportion of the total group is not really feasible — nor indeed, desirable: the lecture
serves other purposes.

The patterns of interaction in a lecture are generally these:

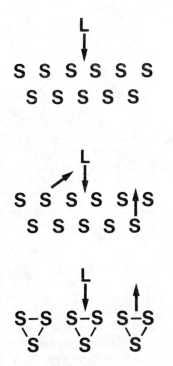

the formal, uninterrupted delivery

the lecture with either spontaneous
questioning during delivery or with
a period of questioning at the end
of the delivery

the lecture with bouts of localised
buzz-group discussion which may
generate questions or comments

The tutorial, when it is conducted on a one-to-one or one-to-two basis, allows
maximum interaction among the people present but the range of views available
is restricted. The small group, or seminar, makes possible the interchange of ideas
on a larger scale and the membership is limited enough still to allow face-to-face
contact so that each member can interact with all the others:

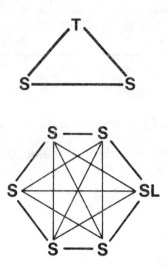

the tutorial

the seminar

1.   *Perceiving the potential*

The distinctive potential of small group work is learning which is based on the expression, exploration and modification of ideas – in cooperative company. People who write about small group work perceive this potential clearly enough, but it does not always seem to be vivid for the practitioners, or perhaps it has been so taken for granted that it has ceased to be a significant factor in decisions about whether or not small group work is appropriate for particular tasks in particular situations.

First, some observations which have been committed to print. Abercrombie (1971, pp. 4-5) says this of the potential of small group work:

'The group system of teaching focuses attention on the interaction between all participants, students and teachers, not on the polarised interaction of a student with a teacher. Like the tutorial, it recognises individual differences, but goes further and not only allows for these differences, but actually exploits them . . . In the tutorial set up, the students' omissions and mistakes are corrected by the teacher; if the teacher is good, the student's store of information tends to match his teacher's in both content and organization. In the group system, the student discovers his strengths and weaknesses himself as he sees his behaviour in the light of others, and he modifies his attitudes or strategies as he sees that there are as many alternatives to them as there are members of the group.'

Brameld (1955, p. 6) also takes up the idea of learning through each other as the characteristic opportunity of small group work: 'Every member can and should be helped to share his resources, whatever they may be.'

In a very different document, prepared by the British Columbia Teachers' Federation (1970), the writer focuses on the individuality of learning which can emerge from a cooperative working group: 'The purpose of group discussion is neither to win an argument nor to amuse oneself. Its purpose is to explore and discover personal meaning.' (p. 2) The writer distinguishes the 'exploratory' or 'learning' group from the 'decision-making' group. The former 'does not seek to convince. Rather, it deals with matters unsolved and seeks to help each member find meanings not existing before.'

There is some agreement here about the process of learning which small group work distinctively supports, but what tasks, thinking first at a very general level, are compatible with this process? Stenhouse (1972, p. 22) neatly carves out three broad categories of task: the task of understanding, the task of applying principles, and the task of applying skills. He gives some examples of what these general tasks would look like in particular subject areas. He mentions applying engineering principles to the design of a particular bridge; applying skills in the design of electronic apparatus to an experimental problem in psychology; understanding, in chemistry, the wave-particle duality in electrons, or, in literature, understanding *Hamlet*.

A particularly interesting passage is his justification of the promoting of understanding as a suitable task for small group work. He points out that understanding, which consists in establishing significant relationships, is both personal and public, and that education is characteristically concerned with public criteria by which understanding can be assessed: 'A personal understanding must be tried out against such criteria.' Here, he aptly catches the tension of small group work which gives it its peculiar advantage: it is the wrestling for balance between personal and public – the search for personal meaning in relation to public criteria, 'public' in terms of, first, the views of other participants in the group and, second, the standards of the discipline which the seminar leader must find a way of representing in the group.

Let us look now at the way practitioners talk about small group work. First, a report of a short conference at which staff and students discussed the pros and cons of introducing small group work more extensively into the medical college's dental school. A staff member gave a paper in which he pointed out the advantages as he saw them:

'i.   The mere acquisition of facts is less important than the acquisition of reasoning power and judgement. The development of both seems to be fostered in small groups . . .

ii.   Cross-proliferation (of ideas) is often missing in teaching systems which do not provide numerous opportunities for group discussion . . .

    iii.　A small group of students, together for three years, generates group spirit of quite a high order . . .

    iv.　Students are not alone in profiting from small group teaching — it has an important role in motivating the teachers to be better teachers . . .

    v.　(Compared with the tutorial system, in small groups) there is a wealth of data . . . which would contribute to the all-important feedback so necessary for the assessment of the students and for the teacher's self-assessment . . .'
(Duckworth, 1970, pp. 16-17)

Physicists constitute the second group of practitioners whose views are presented here. Mainly teachers in higher education, they opted, at a conference, for a session on small group work. During the session they drew up a set of aims for small group work in physics (which, despite their protestation that aims in science teaching would differ from aims in arts teaching, seem remarkably like what one would expect a group of literature and philosophy teachers to produce in similar circumstances):

1.　To help students communicate as physicists. (This aim has to do with language, standards, the structure of knowledge.)

2.　To provide practice in the application of principles.

3.　To encourage the development of appropriate critical standards, and a questioning attitude to evidence.

4.　To extend the range of ideas available to an individual. (It was suggested that the sum of the group's resources was greater than the sum of any individual's resources.)

5.　To help students appreciate that physics is about people.

6.　To provide an opportunity for students to clarify their thinking through talking (using the group as a critical sounding board).

7.　To build opportunities for the critical examination of individual or sub-group assignments.

8.　To encourage familiarity with significant achievements or achievers in physics.

Stenhouse talks about understanding, application of principles and application of skills; the physicists evoke a fourth area of aim: attitudes. Modification of attitude is probably more likely to occur in small group situations where ideas can rub shoulders with other ideas. What the physicists seemed to have in mind was a concern to wean students from the notion that physics is about facts and that the teacher is the infallible purveyor of facts and to encourage them to see that knowledge is provisional and to respond to the controversies that are central to the discipline.

The physicists' first aim, to help students communicate as physicists, defies easy categorisation, perhaps because it amounts to a synthesis of other aims. The concern is to cultivate the characteristic mode of thinking and mode of presentation of the discipline. It includes the acquisition of an appropriate, shared conceptual framework and the refining of appropriate criteria for judgement. It is in a sense a skill, but a complex and sensitive one: the skill of being a physicist. In small group work the student is making increasingly close approximations to being a physicist and these approximations are constantly refined through critical discourse.

A second look at the list above shows that some aims — 5 and 8 in particular, and possibly 3 — could be achieved by learning encounters other than the small group, and we begin to see (from this list and from the one quoted earlier) that there is a gap between the stricter accounts of the distinctive potential of small group work offered by Abercrombie, Brameld and others, and the teachers' and students' conceptualisation of what small groups are good for. Teachers and students — if the lists quoted above are in any way typical — work from a broad set of aspirations which are only loosely derived from the underlying potential of the form. The problem is to harness this potential in specific tasks while bearing in mind the general pay-offs of small group learning that staff and students seem to be interested in.

Most of the statements quoted so far in this section have emphasised the intellectual benefits of small group work but many teachers and students are enthusiastic about small group work for its social value. They might say, for instance, that small groups provide an anchor in the disturbing drift of large institutional life, or that they are territories where individual identities can emerge in some safety, or that they help students to see that their teachers are friendly and caring human beings. One might ask whether it is fair to the distinctive potential of small group work to prize it for its social benefits. It could be argued that intellectual goals are the proper aspiration of a working group — the group exists to serve rather than to please its members. Social ease may well be achieved *through* the development of an effective working relationship, but it is a spin-off or by-product, and it seems important to respect the difference between academic learning groups and social learning (or counselling or therapeutic) groups. The conventions are different, and a blurring of boundaries is likely to baffle student members of any group.

The thesis in this section is that there seems to be a tendency for seminar leaders to justify the use of small group work in general intellectual and social terms and to use a set of broad aspirations as the basis for the selection and planning of group activity. In this process, the distinctive potential of small group work, inter-active learning, is an agreeable but rather insubstantial force and there may be some advantage, when it comes to defining the task of the small group, to return to first principles.

2.   *Covering the syllabus: a threat to the potential of small group work*

A recurrent theme in discussions with students and seminar leaders is pressure for coverage of syllabus — which is commonly felt to be damaging to the potential of small group learning. Here the writers about small group work are very close to the practitioners. A quotation from Stenhouse (1972, p. 22) is followed by a quotation from a teacher of philosophy:

'Every teacher is familiar with a feeling of concern about covering the ground, and students feel this too. I do not believe that participatory small group teaching is an effective way of providing coverage. What is required is individual study, individualised learning programmes and/or lectures. (These do also have other functions.) Nothing is more destructive of participatory small group teaching than concern for coverage in this sense; and any such teaching must take place in a context of coverage supplied by other experiences.'

.   .   .

'With the institution of examinations in the background, it is inevitable that students should worry about 'covering the ground'. If this worry is taken into small groups then it is my impression that discussion can suffer; both students and faculty regard the small group as a means to extending coverage, consolidating information, reinforcing lectures. The leader enters the room with an agenda to be forced through and the students attend with note-pads at the ready. To combat the demon of coverage, we shall test the following moves . . .' (The document from which this passage comes is reproduced in full in Chapter III.)

THE EVIDENCE

1.   *A view of small group work: a professor talks about his approach to small group work in literature*

'It doesn't serve so well for the sheer transmission of knowledge and information, but it does act as a much more efficient stimulus, I think, than lectures . . .

The first week or two I find myself doing most of the talking . . . about the drama-tist or the period or the topic — this often gives me sufficient breathing space at the beginning of the term to draw up a programme of work. This programme consists in appointing a student for each subsequent session of the seminar as chairman of the discussion. I also appoint another student as what I sometimes call secretary, or often scribe, who takes notes of our seminar discussion and at the end of the day produces something not unlike minutes — keeps a written record of the points that have been raised in the discussion which I then generally have typed and duplicated and I give a copy of this to each member of the seminar. So that I've got, as it were, two student officials each week . . . Another one or two students are given a particular topic to prepare for the seminar, perhaps to write an appreciation of a particular drama, or some other topic, to which they then speak . . . Depending on their degree of confidence they either read a paper which they have written, or else they speak from notes which they've drawn up, and all this time the student chairman is in charge of the seminar and I become, as far as I can, a lay member of the seminar . . .

Obviously, until the conventions are understood by the members of the seminar, they tend to turn round to me for the right answer . . . It takes a session or two before my role is properly understood and I try to put this across . . . by making my contribution to the discussion . . . in the interrogative mode rather than in the indicative . . . I think that to learn the conventions of this particular way of running a seminar is difficult the first time through . . . Nevertheless it only requires learning once and then the students more or less know the conventions or the rules of the game . . .

I agree that there is necessarily a kind of lead-in period when — it's like changing up through the gears almost: you start the thing off but you're not into top gear until you've gone through certain intermediate stages. I don't think that these are necessarily lost. I don't think that one must necessarily think of them as being imperfect seminars which have to be endured until you can get the thing going in top gear, but they are preparatory to some extent . . . It very often fails to correspomd with their expectations of a seminar. This is again not without value. It does act as a mental jolt sometimes . . . I think they'd very often be happier if they felt that they could adopt the usual relationship which they are familiar with from school . . .

If a student chairman has to chair the discussion of a particular play, then this is one way of saying to him in effect: "Make sure that you've read it, understood it, and done some work on it" . . . He can't sit silent. Some of the other members of the seminar, on certain occasions, may get away with sitting silently . . . and equally the scribe has to listen very carefully . . . one can only hope that perhaps by asking the appropriate questions, seemingly impersonally but very often directed towards a number of individual members of the seminar group, one can prevent any of them from merely sitting there passively and finishing the hour without having done some intellectual work . . .

I wanted to create many different roles within the seminar group. If the seminar is ten or twelve people then immediately you've got four active people — there are

four officials in any one hour, and the other eight are performing the role of
being seminar members . . . Instead of seeming to stand over them with a stick
and saying "You work, or else", it puts a form of pressure, not unwelcome pressure, on the student to do his work, and the pressure is I suppose the risk of scorn
the following week. And there's also scorn in the seminar if he displays his ignorance when he ought, by virtue of his role, to display familiarity . . . I think the key
role is that of the chairman. Some students, by their lack of experience or by their
make-up, are either not good at conducting the discussion or else they simply fall
down on the job through nerves or through lack of confidence or training or something of that kind; and these are painful occasions. Again I don't think that they're
totally disastrous. As you might imagine, the temptation on my part to jump in
and rescue the situation is great, but I generally manage to resist this. I've come to
see that if I jump in and rescue a discussion that is going badly, then for the rest
of the term I will be forever jumping in and rescuing the discussion . . .

Actually I am prepared and have been prepared to endure awkwardness, silences,
diversions where I could see that the discussion wasn't necessarily going in the
direction that I would want to take it if I were chairman. On the other hand there
are gains from allowing the thing to run like this — gains in the general growth of
confidence to launch out into an analysis, to think on one's feet and not to feel
that this has been done for a teacher who is sitting there preparing to judge performance at the end of it. If one can achieve that atmosphere, that sense . . . then it's
worth while enduring disasters or near disasters . . . I think it very necessary to be
able to carry one's losses in this way without feeling that the thing has gone fundamentally wrong . . .

It has happened that, if we've had rather a sticky session and we've all been groping
for things to say, they will finish with a sense of defeat or frustration. They will
feel that they haven't learned anything or achieved anything. This I tell myself
anyway is in the interests of the future of the seminar . . . What I look for in the
seminar is a good deal of self-propulsion. It must generate its own intellectual
driving force, and not look to me to provide it. Instead of providing the driving
force of the seminar, I provide the navigational corrections. If I feel that it's going
shooting off into space or in the wrong direction, I may certainly be concerned. In
practice I hope that the student chairman will make the navigational correction,
and bring the discussion back to useful areas, but if he doesn't, then preferably by
some oblique, certainly not too blatant or obvious way, I will try to steer the thing
a little . . .

I do provide a fairly formal framework and set out the nature of the programme
and what is expected from the students . . . What I want to avoid are occasions
when we get together and sit down and look at each other and then say "Well,
shall we talk?" . . .

I think it is a little startling and shocking at first, to discover that I'm just going to sit there perhaps silent for the hour. Sometimes this takes a bit of learning and therefore it might be possible simply to alert people in advance that this is going to happen . . .

I think in those disciplines or subjects where there is a cumulative or sequential progression, where in order to move on to the next stage you must thoroughly have mastered the previous stage, probably there the seminar is not necessarily the best device. Maybe this also has to do with whether you are more concerned with the transmission of knowledge or with the stimulation of intellectual skills . . .

I'm less concerned at the end of the day — which means the end of the student's course — if he hasn't covered the subject. This worries me less than if he were to leave so unstimulated by the course that he never really wanted to open another book as long as he lived . . . Whereas somehow to achieve, stimulate, the capacity for independent intellectual exploration, this I would put as absolutely supreme. The capacity and desire for further independent intellectual activities — I ask for no more than this . . .'

CHAPTER II   PROBLEMS OF PARTICIPATION: THE STUDENT'S VIEW

THE ISSUES

This section gives the student's eye view of the problems of participating in small group discussion work. The first part is a brief commentary on what appear to be the main problems and issues. The summary may gain credibility from the documentation which follows in Part II.

The problems are grouped under four broad headings:

1.   making a contribution

2.   understanding the conventions

3.   knowing enough to contribute

4.   being assessed.

1.   *Making a contribution*

Students testify to the difficulty of actually talking in small groups, especially when they have had little previous experience of discussion or are uncertain in what ways learning through discussion in higher education will be different from discussion work in secondary education. Observation of small groups at work (the observations are corroborated by the comments of seminar leaders whose seminars were not monitored by a witness or a camera) shows up the inarticulacy that descends like a shroud on students in small groups, some of whom are known to be confident and resonant speakers in their leisure-time exchanges. Within the academic walls of seminar rooms many students become monosyllabic mumblers — and a fluent individual can quickly take possession of the discourse.

It's easy to underestimate the difficulty a student can have in taking responsibility for his own interventions — anticipating the end of another speaker's contribution, seizing a silence — when for much of his secondary education he has signalled his readiness to contribute by raising his hand and been cued in by his teacher. Sometimes one sees a punitive device being operated — the teacher calls on a student precisely because she suspects that the student is inattentive or unprepared. In small group discussion, students have to learn to balance courtesy with self-interest and at the same time be mindful of the need to listen as well as to frame and feed in their own contributions.

One difficulty derives from common assumptions about the linear nature of discussion. By the time a nervous student has put his thoughts together, and had a silent rehearsal, they have lost their aptness. The discussion has moved on and he keeps his silence.

A different tactic is employed by the less sensitive scholar who has difficulty in getting his toe in at the door of the discussion. He will store up his remarks and when he does win the floor will unburden himself of a number of points, not necessarily related to each other nor to the present focus of the group's attention. The logic of discussion is threatened as participants are offered a number of new starting points, some of them pursuing lines of argument which the group has moved beyond. Of course, the group can deal with the 'hoarder' by ignoring his ideas and picking up the thread at the point where he intervened — but he has the satisfaction of having said his piece, whereas the student who stops short at the moment of intervention, because he senses that he has missed the logic of the discourse, may be building up anxieties that make it increasingly difficult for him to contribute. There is something to be said for the strategy by which a seminar leader makes an opportunity for *every* member of a group to say something early on in a seminar so that the fears that attend the first utterance are allayed. Thereafter, the seminar leader will have to decide whether a student has a right to remain silent — silence does not necessarily mean that no learning is going on — or whether, given the distinctive potential of small group work as outlined by Abercrombie (page 4), a student has a responsibility *to other students* to make a contribution, so that each gives as well as takes.

Another major difficulty for undergraduates in small group discussion work is in becoming proficient in the language of their discipline. It is likely that they learn what discourse is appropriate by taking the seminar leader, or the lecturer, as a language model. It would be unfortunate therefore if in their first term a system of tutorless small groups were organised on the grounds that students will talk more comfortably when the staff member is not present. This may be so (see the discussion of Powell's study on pp. 99-102), and the dilemma then is whether confidence in talking in an informal register will facilitate the acquisition of the appropriate academic register at a later stage, or whether early familiarity with the sound and structures of the academic discourse is a better basis for confident participation in formal discussion work.

2.   *Understanding the conventions*

Video-tapes of undergraduates at their first seminars show how guarded the students are about making moves. In one seminar, identical cardboard boxes (designed to demonstrate wave-particle duality in electrons and containing an un-identified moving object) stood at each place round the seminar table. It was remarkable that students did not feel free to touch or lift — let alone shake — the box until they had been cajoled into so doing by the seminar leader, whose enquiry approach to learning could only proceed in relation to speculation about the contents of the box — which was the sole input of the seminar!

Students often confess to being uncertain as to how to respond in a seminar if the leader does not lecture to them and it is noticeable how frequently in their early experience of small group work students resort to note-taking — but invariably recording only points made by the seminar leader! Rarely do they commit to paper (seen presumably as an aid to examination revision) comments made by a fellow student.

There are particular conventions that students say they are uneasy about. For instance, how far one should go in acknowledging confusion or misunderstanding — or whether in a higher education seminar there is a tacit agreement that one disguises uncertainty or ignorance and talks only from relative certainty. Students can also be bewildered by the conventions which surround the student paper. What exactly is required — especially when a paper has to serve both as a stimulus for discussion and as the basis of a written assignment? And what is required of the student when he has finished presenting his paper: is he one of the group, or does he maintain the role of 'speaker' — and does he share some responsibility for the management of the group with the seminar leader?

The student has also to learn to read the settings in which he finds himself (given that seminar styles often differ from tutor to tutor). What behaviours are signalled by a room with an even arrangement of upright chairs around a bare central table? Is one of the chairs the tutor's? And even if the chairs are indistinguishable in shape, size, colour and comfort, one place will tend to be perceived -- perhaps because it is near the blackboard — as the tutor's and the convention clearly is to keep one's distance at first. It is the latecomer who gets trapped in the seat which it is very difficult to talk from (until, that is, students are weaned from the habit of addressing all their remarks to the seminar leader) — the seat next to the seminar leader.

The student may also have to interpret the cues for behaviour in the very different seminar setting of the seminar leader's study: are the exchanges more informal when the seating is more ad hoc? Does one call the seminar leader by her first name? Can one smoke? If the social setting seems to demand some casual preliminary chat, how does one know when the seminar itself has started? Does it automatically start on time (in fact, a rather rare occurrence), or is it related to the arrival of the last member, or will the seminar leader signal the opening — or is this the responsibility of the student whose turn it is to give a paper?

The dilemmas described so far under the headings 'making a contribution', and 'understanding the conventions' relate to an anxiety that is essentially about making a fool of oneself in front of the seminar leader and in front of one's peers (students have said that a common inhibitor early in seminar work is the thought that one may have fewer 'A' levels and lower grades than one's peers).

3. *Knowing enough to contribute*

Students frequently attribute their reticence in discussion to sheer uncertainty about the agenda. There may have been no clear statement of the topic under discussion and the criteria for deciding what is relevant belong therefore to the seminar leader who, students tend to assume, must have some notion of the purpose of the seminar in *her* head. Students are also concerned about their ignorance. How much does one need to 'know' in order to participate in discussion, and at what point do individual differences in knowledge feed the understanding of the participants as opposed to stultifying them — making them feel 'lost' or inadequate? This phenomenon is often apparent when a student becomes dominant who has a particular vein of curiosity or expertise; the seminar leader may take him on in specialist dialogue which will effectively cut out participation by other members of the group.

One way through the knowledge dilemma is for the seminar leader to establish common ground in the group by providing copies of a text for students to read before or during the session, or to specify the preparation. The responsibility for not being prepared is then the student's. Of course, there is always the hopeful excuse — like the classic non-deceiver offered by a student in a seminar on Chekhov's The Cherry Orchard: 'By the time I got to the library the only books left were in Russian.'

Students also acknowledge a sense of inadequacy when the seminar leader sets a style of fairly aggressive intellectual challenge. They do not feel that they know enough to come back at her and will protect themselves by silence — this can sometimes extend to a protective obstinacy which involves the whole group. In fact, silence can be a strong group weapon.

4. *Being assessed*

The seminar, ideally, is a place where people can take risks with ideas. Risk-taking is more likely to occur in a secure structure and the security of the seminar is sometimes threatened for students by uncertainty about assessment. Are they being assessed? And, if so, on what? The obvious conclusion, in the absence of any explanation of the assessment procedure, is that they are being assessed on their spoken contributions (frequency? length? or the more elusive concept of quality?).

Students have also expressed anxiety about informal assessment: will the seminar leader tell her colleagues what 'x' said in the seminar and, if so, because it was absurd or — and this seems a greater source of unease — because it was ideologically unacceptable? In short, will the values behind the contributions be taken into account as well as their logic or their relation to evidence?

So far in this section, anxieties and uncertainties that underlie some of the problems of participation have been outlined on the assumption that university and college staff who are accustomed to holding seminars may need to renew their sense of what small group work can feel like for the new undergraduate. The new seminar leader may herself be suffering anxieties and uncertainties (these do not always go unnoticed by students — see the quotations that follow) and she may well be so preoccupied with her own apprenticeship to the form that she fails to notice the feelings of other members of the group.

Of course, the seminar leader, new or experienced, may well argue that coping with the slings and arrows of undergraduate academic life is the responsibility of the students (or the students supported by the counselling service) but one can also argue that many of the uncertainties derive from insufficient briefing or inadequate definition of the task — and these are surely the responsibilities of the seminar leader. The next chapter will consider what, within her strictly academic role, the seminar leader might do to increase the opportunities for participation in small group discussion.

THE EVIDENCE

1.   *First year students comment on small group work*

Twelve students agreed to be interviewed before the start of an experiment in small group work in chemistry. The twelve volunteers were interviewed in groups of two to four students. There is no claim that the comments reproduced below are representative of what the total group of sixty felt. There was, however, considerable similarity of emphasis and tone among the students interviewed. The quotations have been selected to indicate the range of issues raised as the students talked about their experience of small group work in the first year of their course.

The comments are roughly grouped under three general headings:

a.   general attitude and the habit of non-participation

b.   factors affecting participation

c.   techniques that staff and students might use to encourage participation

a.   *Attitude of students to small group work and the habit of non-participation*

'If you read about it it sounds very good. Some people every week go into a room and talk about the previous week's lectures; it sounds great but when you actually come to do it you sit around without saying anything and the seminar leader isn't quite sure how to get them started anyway and this carries on for about twenty weeks — two terms — and you begin to think it's not such a good idea.'

'In our first year if anybody asks a question like in a lecture theatre or anything like that you just get no reaction at all . . . It's always been like that. I don't know why. It usually happens, you know . . . I just seem to sit there.'

'I don't feel I get very much out of seminars. I feel it's just something you go to. You just have to sit there and go away.'

b.   *Factors affecting participation*

Compulsory attendance:

'Yes, you tend to look at them rather as something which you have to go to just because you have to rather than because they do any good for you.'

'There's eight seminars in each subject and you have to attend six of them to get a mark . . . so a lot of people go just to get the mark. They give you an hour exam if you miss a certain number. It's not so much a threat for missing them as an option — at least, so faculty say.'

The content:

'In a science seminar, though, you are dealing basically with facts and it doesn't really leave a great deal open to discussion. It's just you know the facts or you don't, to a large extent.'

Shyness, anxiety and distrust:

'You are thrown into a room with people you don't know and you sort of tend to be shy, you know, in coming out with problems and I suppose as you go through the course the seminar group will get better, providing it stays as one entity.'

'The group seems to split up after a seminar; they're not a social group outside the seminar.'

'I don't know why but anyway you can never get any positive reaction from the seminar group . . . People don't just speak of their own accord unless they have a direct question because they don't like the other people to think that they are being clever.'

(The main problem in talking is) 'who's going to answer first, I would think, more than anything. All looking at each other to see who is going to say something, first. Relying on somebody else and nobody does, and by the time you sort of think of it you think "Oh it's too late now, you know; might as well keep quiet." '

'Well one minute they'll be saying this idea of the seminar is to help you understand the basics and then you'll make a basic statement and they'll say "You ought to know this by now''. And of course if you don't know it they tend to sort of jump on you.'

'We tend to keep quiet so they try to get their own back.'

'. . . things may get back; they may discuss what people have said in seminars. I don't suppose it would happen but it's in the back of people's minds before they speak.'

The seminar leader's inexperience:

'. . . unless your seminar leader is experienced in sort of seminar teaching, it is very difficult for him to make the seminar really operative, really make it work.'

'Yes, I think if they are more inexperienced they tend to come in with something pre-planned. They come in and start and end when the seminar finishes . . . well not always but in general they are worse seminars, you know. I wouldn't say the younger seminar leaders always do this. It depends on how experienced they are actually; what their personalities are.'

'It just stops. Half way through the seminar it just stops. Nobody speaks for two minutes. (Interviewer asks what happens when there is a silence.) Very little. The seminar leader breaks the silence. These silences can be rather draughty at some times . . . The seminar leader can't stand silences. He is always the one who breaks it.'

'Well, we had one this term; he looked so nervous when he was taking us, you know, I thought he was going to die of fright. Of course we didn't help any, not being very talkative. Sometimes you get pulled to pieces of course.'

'One we have he always brings a book in and sort of looks up in the book some of the things. He's not completely sure what he's doing himself. He's a good laugh.'

'Start the seminar with a more experienced person to get them in the right attitude for the whole course. You could then put postgraduates on to them and the group would know what to expect more.'

Her capacity to manage the follow-up seminar to a lecture:

'One tends to find that the seminar leader will just say "Any questions? Right. Well I've got something for you to do." '

'I think very few people actually read through a lecture and go to a seminar with any particular problem, you know. The seminar leader comes in and says "Any problems?" and there's just a rustling of paper as you read through the last lecture quickly ... It usually ends up that nobody has any specific points ... He's got a printed sheet typed out ... Well since we never talk it's probably quite a good idea.'

'Sometimes it's useful being in the lecturer's seminar because you can quote what he has said. If it's another member of faculty that's taking you for the seminar they don't know exactly what has been said in the lecture.'

Her dominance and the authority of his knowledge:

'Some lecturers come in and they just start, you know, like another lecture in the seminar.'

'I suppose it would be best if the seminar leader spoke as little as possible. That would be ideal, but it just doesn't happen like that. It could if you got on to something that was really interesting, but things are a bit beyond everybody's grasp I think, so they don't really know it and are not really interested in it.'

'The point is we don't know enough really to answer back and do much talking ourselves ...'

(The tutor sits) 'usually in front of the blackboard. Somewhere central, in a rather central position.'

Her attitude to teaching:

(They are here) 'primarily to do research; teaching is just a side line. (Interviewer asks if students get angry.) Yes, because this is a University which is meant for teaching.'

Problems of organisation: size and stability of groups:

'The seminar sessions are one and a half hours; I think personally that's too long.'

'If the students spoke up a bit more than they did they'd get more out of it, but we don't do. I think the groups are too big, but there again sometimes seminar leaders don't prod enough.'

'Sometimes only five people turn up; it's really a good seminar. There's not many people to make a fool of yourself in front of.'

'You get used to the way people act in a seminar or the way they talk and if they kept changing all the time you would be a bit on edge I would think, not knowing what to expect. You also get somebody who keeps speaking up all the time, like canaries, and you get to rely on them to say something.'

c.   *Techniques that staff and students might use to encourage participation*

Staff:

'We had one last term. He sat in the corner of the room and just wrote a problem on the board and we took it in turns to do this problem and, in a way, worked through the principles and it was very good. I liked that seminar. We didn't have to do much talking, in a way, but discussing it, and he was just sort of sitting on the side line and bringing in ideas. I think it is better if they get you to come up to the board and do something.'

'I think if the seminar leader at the beginning of the seminar sort of brought up the problem and went to each person to get them to say something about the problem, you know, give them a chance, then they'd get somebody starting to talk and you know eventually everybody would start talking, but if you start off silent you just carry on silent through the whole thing.'

Students:

'Some fault lies with them and some fault lies with us.'

'Try and be as cooperative as possible with the seminar leaders. Try and make some preparation and be prepared to speak up. Possibly try and think up some questions that are not straightforward but which are likely to bring forward a bit of discussion.'

(These extracts were reproduced, with permission, in *Small Group Teaching: Selected Papers,* a compilation by the Nuffield Foundation's Group for Research and Innovation in Higher Education. For a parallel set of comments by first year students at a college of education, see Bridges, 1975.)

CHAPTER III THE SEMINAR LEADER'S ROLES AND RESPONSIBILITIES

THE ISSUES

1.   *The problem of authority*

In small group work there is evidence to suggest that the central problem in the relationship between staff and students is the nature of authority. The authority of the seminar leader is many-sided: it derives from knowledge (she is 'a teacher', she is probably conducting research in her own field, she may be writing about her ideas), and it derives from her status as a representative of the institution. In R.S. Peters' terms, she is both 'an authority' and 'in authority'. The teacher is 'in authority' as a representative of her institution. This authority is consciously present to her students: she is seen as defining the task and the situation in which it will be tackled. (Stenhouse, 1972, p. 19) Her authority is reinforced by her responsibility as internal examiner. The teacher is 'an authority' by virtue of her knowledge and expertise in her discipline. This authority may be furbished by academic reputation as a speaker and writer, and is likely to be strengthened by age and charisma. Moreover, the teacher is likely to be seen as an insider in the academic world at large, at home with journals, committees, conferences, controversies and debates. 'The consequence of this authority position of the teacher is that students brought up in our system expect him to play the role of instructor in the sense that they expect him to take responsibility for their learning. They assume an attitude of dependence. Now there are occasions — even in small groups — when instruction is appropriate. But there are also many occasions when students have to accept responsibility for their own learning, to develop autonomy as scholars, and hence to learn to use the tutor as a consultant and guide rather than as an instructor. It is in this context that participatory small groups are appropriate ... All in all the teacher cannot escape the responsibilities of a leadership position and the problems in the area of authority-dependency which this sets up.' (Stenhouse, 1972, p. 20) The authority — or power — of the teacher is singled out for discussion by a speaker at a symposium on teaching methods organised by the Dental School of the London Hospital Medical College:

'There are certain teachers who may find it hard not to be power-figures in their groups, in the way that they might have to be in lectures. Student productivity has been related to this notion of the power-figure and it has been claimed that productivity is low when:

—   the teacher appears very knowledgeable,

—   the teacher talks a good deal,

—   the students are ridiculed if they make mistakes or suggest wild ideas.

Conversely, student productivity will probably be higher when:

—   the teacher defines problem areas, rather than solutions,

—   the teacher shows that he does not see himself as infallible,

—   the teacher talks less,

—   the teacher encourages students who introduce creative or original ideas.'
(Duckworth, 1970, p. 18)

Clearly, the authority of the seminar leader can inhibit participation in a variety
of ways. Students may be beguiled into adopting the role of appreciative listeners,
sitting at the feet of the expert rather than confronting each other and learning
through a fuller exchange of ideas. They may interpret their task as one of learning what is in the *teacher's* mind rather than as an enquiry into knowledge itself.
Students may become cautious in the presence of an authority lest they appear
ingenuous and invite correction.

Stenhouse argues that if a teacher handles her authority unselfconsciously, as a
matter of habit, she usually induces a relatively passive dependence in her students.
The achievement of independence in learning requires conscious effort by all
concerned and a respect for procedure. If conventions for the group's learning
are not made explicit, the students' only recourse for discovering what behaviour
is appropriate is to observe the seminar leader and build theories about what she
is up to. In this way the seminar leader's position as focal point is reinforced and
the students will become teacher-oriented rather than task-oriented.

Some examples of 'contracts' are reproduced later. They were drawn up by
seminar leaders. Their function is to define and limit the authority of the seminar
leader and to provide criteria through which the group can discuss her contribution.
The purpose of the contracts is to help the group cope with and make the most of
the staff member in ways that are consistent with the learning potential of small
group work.

The notion of 'contract' underlines the formality of this kind of teaching, whereas
small group work is often seen by students and teachers as an informal event —
coffee-on-the-carpet in the curious sanctuary of the teacher's academic pad. The
position taken in this book is that effective learning in small groups is facilitated by
formal structures and procedures. Indeed, informality is generally likely to *increase*
dependence on the staff member: in socially ambiguous situations, such as the
seminar in the seminar leader's study, cues are taken from the seminar leader,
initiatives are expected of her — students become the followers of her fashion.

2.   Some roles open to a seminar leader

What range of roles is open to the seminar leader? As a result of observation we would list these: the instructor, the participant, the model, the devil's advocate, the chairman, the consultant. The contributions of the seminar leader who plays the part of instructor or participant are likely to be closely related to her individual perceptions and values; as model or as devil's advocate, her contributions are likely to reflect the views traditionally represented in the discipline; as chairman or consultant her interventions are likely to be largely procedural.

The instructor: in small group work some instructional input is often essential. It can be helpful if the seminar leader explains that she intends to lecture for a limited period, say ten minutes, and that discussion of her contribution will follow. The dilemma is whether the seminar leader can manage to provide the instruction in her own person without forging dependency relationships that may obstruct the interdependent learning that is distinctive of small group work. What may be at stake is the group's capacity to scrutinise the instructor's input as critically as they might be expected to examine input from any other source. Where the seminar leader's authority is such that any instruction is received with uncritical acceptance, it is likely to be difficult for the group to move from listening into discussion. The danger is when students accept that the teacher as instructor has 'a right to be sure' (Israel Scheffler). Seminar leaders who hope for discussion at the end of a long period of exposition from them might ask themselves the following question: 'Do teachers always realise the paralysing and stupefying effect that a flood of talk has upon the mind?'
(Mason, quoted in *Resources for Learning,* p. 126)

The participant: the participant seminar leader is a resource in the discussion even as students are resources. She contributes in her own person. Her Scylla is authority (her views being given undue attention, but uncritically); her Charybdis is vulnerability (her values being given undue attention, and critically). The difficulty of the role lies in the perceived or intended relationship between 'teaching' and 'participation':

'In teaching, the teacher is revealing his reasons for the beliefs he wants to transmit and is thus, in effect, submitting his own judgement to the critical scrutiny and evaluation of the student; he is fully engaged in the dialogue by which he hopes to teach, and is thus risking his own beliefs, in lesser or greater degree, as he teaches.'
(Scheffler, 1965, pp. 11-12)

The participant role needs careful definition to the group, and it might be interesting to speculate, in this context, on the force of the commonly cited description of the seminar leader in the small group as 'primus inter pares'. The elegance of the Latin probably protects the phrase from the scrutiny it deserves.

The model: the model role is where the seminar leader presents herself as an historian, a physicist, a philosopher, a critic of literature. Her moves and responses reflect the standards of the discipline and the characteristic ways of thinking – of perceiving and selecting data, and of organising experience. The student learns from the historian what it is like to study and to talk as an historian. The role requires that the seminar leader and the students subject their performance to the same criteria and that the criteria are derived from the discipline that provides the common territory for their work. The danger is in the seminar room becoming a theatre, the seminar leader, academically well-rehearsed and confident of her lines, inviting individual students to pit their wits against hers, calling for contributions and skilfully demolishing the arguments, taking on the image of the star rather than of the self-critical thinker.

The devil's advocate: the devil's advocate is a more commonly and consciously held role. It is one in which the seminar leader takes on the group, challenging students, debating their positions, shifting her ground, almost acrobatically, in order to achieve a new line of attack. The group needs to be robust.

The devil's advocate surrenders the expression of personal commitment to general skill in argument. The role is usually justified in terms of stirring the group, or as one seminar leader put it, engineering dissent. The authority of the seminar leader is invested in quick-witted skills rather than in knowledge (except that she is familiar with and can speak from a range of positions that are traditionally held within the discipline). The role can be about cleverness rather than wisdom. It is one in which the seminar leader is generally bound to win.

The chairman: or more specifically, and in areas of controversy, the neutral chairman. The neutral chairman is one who trains herself to exclude the expression of personal opinion from discussion on the grounds that undue weight is likely to be given to her contributions. The role is difficult to achieve but it is in a stalwart tradition. Charlotte Mason, educational reformer of the nineteenth century, was within it:

'She avoided expressions of personal opinion lest they should act like 'suggestion' on those who loved her. She distrusted personal influence as limiting and belittling the person influenced and she steadily set her face against any form of personal influence over any with whom she came in contact . . . she would not deliver those she loved from the growing pains of thinking for themselves.'
(Quoted in *Resources for Learning*, p. 128)

The creative contribution of the chairman to the work of the small group is her concern for procedures that promote independence of student learning.
The neutral chairman, at best, communicates high expectations of student performance. It is a task-centred, rather than person-centred role. 'The goal . . . is discip-

lined understanding; that is the process as well.' (Bruner, 1960, p. 196). The seminar leader cannot be both chairman and source of information; adequate alternative sources of data need to be available to the group. The seminar leader, as chairman, is strictly 'in authority', not allowing herself to contribute as 'an authority'. The role is difficult for students to adjust to in so far as they expect instruction. It is difficult for the seminar leader in that while she attempts to hold back in discussion she must accept responsibility for relevance and standards and must learn to mediate standards largely through critical questioning.

There are of course opponents of the neutral chairman role. But Brameld's position – that the teacher *must* make known her view to the group – requires an equally mature response from the students. He is aware of the problem of authority, but builds in different safeguards:

'In the first place, he owes it to the group to indicate his own preferences frankly and clearly, while yet making apparent in the way he operates that these preferences are continually subject to reconsideration, modification, or even disapproval. Whether such indication should be made almost at the beginning of deliberations, or in the course of group interaction and growth, depends both upon the nature of the group and upon the type of issue under consideration . . . The principle that the leader should be forthright is, however, the same regardless of variation in the character of the group. And one of the chief values of this principle is that members are alerted to and made more critical of any weighted efforts the leader may make to guide the process in his own preferred direction. In the second place, the ethical leader does everything he can to provide opportunity for expression of feeling and opinion by those who differ with him.'
(1955, p. 7)

Indeed, some people may feel that the roles of consultant and chairman are incompatible with a view of the positive responsibilities of a teacher. This is an issue for debate and empirical study in the climate and context of one's own institution and classroom.

The consultant: this role requires that students learn how to make the most of what the staff member can offer: the initiatives lie with them, but if students are to take them effectively, they require a framework which makes clear the nature of their task, the resources available, and the accessibility of the consultant. Is she 'on call' in case the group hits a problem, or is she the figure who automatically appears to offer exegesis at the end of the session? One temptation is to use the consultant role as a way out of management difficulties and not primarily for its educational advantage: it is a way of running four small groups concurrently and with only one member of staff who wanders round, like a policeman on his beat, to check that all is well. The title of consultant implies a sort of on-tap wisdom. One of the problems for the seminar leader who is attracted by this role (rather than the organisational arrangements it implies) is ensuring that she does not *make* herself seem needed — to what extent does she encourage students to manage on their own? Are her encounters with students genuinely productive for their learning or are they a means of checking up on whether the work has been done?

.   .   .

A typology is perhaps of limited value unless the roles carry sufficiently detailed specifications to serve as models — or unless the incumbent is prepared, having identified from among the types the closest approximation to her present practice, to work out, for herself, the implications for seminar procedure. An outline typology has one advantage — it serves to remind one of the variety of approaches possible within an institution and even within a department — and the variety, therefore, that students encounter and have to learn to respond to. Fortunately, secondary education, with its traditionally fragmented timetable and kaleidoscope of teachers and teaching styles, ensures that students entering higher education are pretty adaptable. What is important, therefore, is not to diminish the variety but to ensure that each seminar leader offers an explanation of her approach, or behaves consistently, or both.

3.   *Basic responsibilities of the seminar leader*

Five areas of responsibility, which are both basic and, at least in broad outline, non-controversial, are discussed here.

> a.   Responsibility for the definition and communication of purpose, task and agenda. (This does not necessarily mean that the seminar leader must always determine the agenda herself. Of course, she may do this, but her overriding responsibility is for ensuring that there *is* a commonly understood and agreed focus and sense of direction, whether the immediate agenda is drawn up by the group as a whole or by different members, or sub-groups, in turn.)

> b.   Responsibility for ensuring that there is common ground as the basis for discussion. (This responsibility is really for the oversight of main sources of input for the discussion or activity that is the mode of enquiry of the group.)

> c.   Responsibility for clarifying issues of assessment. (That is, whether or not the seminar is subject to continuous assessment, and if so, what is the mode of assessment.)

> d.   Responsibility for time-keeping.

> e.   Responsibility for maintaining the spirit of small group work. (That is, for respecting its potential and characteristics as a particular form of

learning.)

a.   *Responsibility for the definition and communication of purpose, task and agenda*

It seems crucial in small group work that neither procedures nor knowledge should become the private bounty of the teacher, dispersed or disclosed at will. Energy can be wastefully spent in guessing what is in the teacher's mind, whether opinions (what students ought to be thinking) or procedures (what students ought to be doing). Symptoms of such dependence are when the group exhibit behaviours that say 'what do you want us to do?' instead of exploring what it is appropriate to do in terms of the task.

It may be that the seminar leader, at least initially, should accept responsibility for the general design of the sessions and for ensuring that the group as a whole comprehends the design. She must be able to help students take advantage of what the small group can offer.

Several questions seem to be important:

— what common perceptions do students in the group have, at the outset of the course, of the nature and demands of small group work?

— do students have a realistic sense of what might be achieved through the course of seminars as a whole?

— do students understand what each session is to be about, and, more specifically, what the task of each session is?

— do students know clearly what reading or thinking is necessary in preparation for each meeting — and, perhaps even more important, do they see preparation as a requirement imposed by the seminar leader or as an investment which is in the interests of the group's progress?

There seem, from observation, to be four common ways of defining the area of study for each session (this is not necessarily the same as defining the task):

— the overall theme is determined by the seminar leader at the beginning of term and the weekly topics and problems are listed, often with suggested or required reading. Students may present papers on the topics;

— the topic for each session is determined by the group at the end of the preceding session;

—   lines of attack are identified by individuals at the start of a meeting
(for instance, when discussion centres on problems raised by students
who have heard a common lead lecture);

—   lines of enquiry emerge during the session itself. (In this approach it
may well be important for the chairman to catch significant issues
that are thrown up and to hold the group to an exploration of them.)

In whatever way the task of individual sessions is defined, a crucial problem is that
of building continuities from session to session. A sense of continuity may, of
course, be created — or fabricated — by the seminar leader's summary at the start
of each session of 'what we did last time' but this slender convention can mean
that continuity is an artefact of the notebook rather than a force carried in the
minds of the group.

b.   *Responsibility for ensuring that there is common ground as the basis for
discussion*

The structure of small group meetings is largely shaped by devices to secure
adequate input for discussions. The Hale Committee comments in 1964: 'The
introduction of more teaching by discussion is beneficial only when it can be
matched by a corresponding increase in the amount of private study done by the
student . . .' (University Grants Committee Ch. VIII) A major anxiety among
seminar leaders is the unreliability of student preparation. This does not necessarily imply irresponsibility among students; they may well be uncertain what
consititutes appropriate preliminary work for a small group meeting or they may
find that any preparation that they do themselves is overridden by the agenda
brought to the meeting by the seminar leader. The Hale Committee offers a
solution: 'Perhaps the most effective way of getting students to do preparatory
work is to set them an essay or other written exercise to be prepared for discussion.'
(Ch. VII) The student paper is still widely used in small group work as a device for
securing common ground. Other common devices for securing common ground
for the discussion are the preliminary lecture and the whole-group event.

— the student paper

By this we mean a presentation by one student to the rest of the group. Students
who present papers may value the opportunity they provide for the disciplining
and shaping of their own thinking. Students who receive papers are often adversely
critical — but teachers seem to have acquired a fondness for the convention which
ensures that well-founded criticisms do not give rise to alternative ways of providing
input for discussion.

One problem is that the student paper often has to serve ends that are, in practice,
incompatible. The paper may have to function both as a stimulus to discussion and
as the first draft (and sometimes final draft) of a written essay which will be assessed.

If the presentation is to culminate in an essay, then the small group meeting might usefully be regarded as the testing ground for ideas; the formal paper would then be written up in the light of the discussion. A formal piece of continuous writing is not really appropriate as a curtain-raiser to discussion. The mode is awkward. The paper is likely to be too long and too well substantiated for members of the group to make an adequate spontaneous response or it may be too finished or closed to invite challenge in discussion. In addition, seminar leaders familiar with the ground covered underestimate the difficulties student listeners may have in following an oral presentation. It might be helpful for a student paper reader to prepare, in advance, a duplicated outline of his presentation as a framework for the group's listening. Of course, some students will feel more competent and confident in presenting a fully written paper than in talking to notes. In this case, the paper may need to be broken up so that passages can be discussed — what is at stake then is whether the paper reader is expecting interruptions. Nothing can be more irritating and undermining to a paper reader who has attempted to prepare a coherent argument than to have the seminar leader continuously pecking at his presentation. The conventions for giving and receiving a paper clearly need to be agreed by the group.

The student paper is likely to be more effective if its expected function in the discussion is clear to the writer and to the listeners. It might offer data for discussion or it might be offering a framework for discussion: the first approach requires a critical response in terms of the nature of evidence; the second assumes that listeners will relate knowledge they already possess to the issues identified in the paper. The group may need to know in advance whether the reader intends to present a personal synthesis or evaluation, or is attempting to reflect or summarise common positions in the field.

A poor seminar paper is likely to lose the group and put pressure on the seminar leader to come in and conduct a salvage operation — possibly by moving into an instructional role. On the other hand, a very good seminar paper (good in terms of its scholarship) may also lose the group — not in interest, but because it places ideas beyond the students' grasp. The small group discussion may then become a dialogue between the student paper reader and the seminar leader.

The poor paper may expose the student to personal criticism and the seminar leader may have to make fine judgements: what the student is protected from he cannot be helped with — but harsh exposures of ignorance or incompetence may make a student reluctant to risk his ideas in later discussions. And if the group is loyal to persons rather than to standards, and is tolerant of a poor paper, the critical function may be left entirely to the seminar leader. Her authority as holder of knowledge and critic will then be heavily reinforced.

The student paper reader may be uncertain of his role in the group after the paper has been presented. Does he maintain a special role? How does the action move

from direct questioning of him to general discussion, and what part does he play
in the discussion? There are sometimes signs of competition between the seminar
leader and the student paper reader for the chairman's role. In one observed discussion, the student paper reader was given a chair higher than the chairs of other
members of the group, yet his physically different position was not reinforced by
his role in the period after the reading of the paper, and his awkwardness was
apparent in his attempt to shrink to the common height of his peers!

– the small group as follow-up to a lecture

A lecture that precedes the small group meeting, and which all students should
have attended, provides common ground for the seminar activity. The task of the
small group meeting is to work through individual students' misunderstandings or
insights. In some meetings the aim may be restricted to the clarification and illumination of points made in a lecture; in others, the seminar leader may seek to move
the group through misunderstandings in the territory of the lecture and on to new
ground, or at least to provide a wider range of settings to test the group's compet-
ence in the application of the principles derived from the lecture.

In small group meetings which follow a lecture, the main difficulty is likely to lie
in the tension between the interests of individuals and of the group as a whole.
First, it may be necessary to legitimize the expression of misunderstanding, perhaps
by the seminar leader recalling stumbling blocks that she faced as a student, or by
her recollecting problems that other groups have encountered. Various issues snag
the next step: how do students locate the problems that need explication? Are they
formally given time for this at the beginning of the seminar or at the end of the
lecture, or are they expected to make their own time for revision and to arrive
ready to detail their difficulties to the group? Observation shows, however, that
at the start of the seminar there is generally a period of hasty recall, with busy
shuffling of notes, in response to the seminar leader's open invitation: 'Was there
anything you wanted to discuss?' If no problems are offered by the group, does
the seminar leader assume the initiative and present a set of anticipated problems
to test the group's complacence? It is only a short move, once it is known that the
seminar leader keeps a contingency plan, for the group to avoid the trouble of
searching out stale difficulties and wait instead for the seminar leader to provide
the agenda for them.

If the students have problems that they want to raise, the seminar leader will face
some procedural decisions:

—   Is she to tackle a problem as it is offered, or would it be more efficient of
     her, and sensitive, to collect an agenda of problems so that she can be mind-
     ful of sequence and of the allocation of time to particular items? In this way,
     a student would know at the outset that his problem had secured a place on
     the agenda, even though it might not be the first to be discussed.

— Is the seminar leader to enquire how many students share a particular
problem? (She must then think how majority and minority needs can be
accommodated in a group situation.) Will a group allow the needs of an
individual to dominate the agenda, or how can acceptable compromises
be made?

— Does the effort at clarification thrust the seminar leader into a central,
authoritative position, or can she encourage students to clarify the issues
and approaches for each other?

The importance of agenda in relation to individual and group interests is under-
lined in a strategy described by Epstein (1972, pp. 4-5).

She would have teachers pose a question, formally: 'Is there anything from the
lecture that you would like us to go over in the group?' Then she waits. 'After
the question is asked and there is some silence the students begin to respond . . .
As the students respond the teacher writes each response verbatim on the board.
She makes no comment. She is merely the recorder for the students' responses.
Occasionally, the teacher asks a student if she has written his response correctly . . .
After six or seven responses have been recorded, there is silence. The teacher says
nothing. She merely waits . . . If the silence continues beyond ten or twelve seconds,
she may repeat the question and then wait. The responses will probably start again
. . . A twenty second silence probably signifies that the census is complete.' The
teacher ensures that all members of the group can see, or have taken a copy of,
the agenda.

A less usual relationship between lecture and small group is one in which the
sequence is reversed: in the small group meeting, the seminar leader identifies
issues that she needs to give attention to in her *follow-up* lecture. I have only met
this practice once, in a department where the teacher acted as seminar leader to
three parallel groups, meeting each in turn on the first four days of the week. On
the Friday he gave a follow-up lecture. Preparation was inevitably a strain — he
could not work with confidence from last year's notes because his aim was to
explore questions and issues raised that week in the seminars. Indeed, the final
source of data which determined the emphasis of his lecture was a meeting on the
day before he was due to give the lecture.

— group event

In this approach the content of the small group discussion derives from an event
or task that the group as a whole is engaged in. The event or task would generally
occur within the small group meeting itself. The strength of this design is that it
provides, *in situ*, common ground for the group's learning. The experience might
be one of reading a scene from a play, watching an audio-visual presentation of
material, conducting an experiment.

Sub-group tasks that are undertaken *between* small group meetings and are reported to the group as a whole are perhaps closer in strategy to the student paper presentation than to the whole group event, but there is one difference. The sharing by three or more students of responsibility for providing input for the discusion ensures that it is not only the individual paper reader and the seminar leader who are capable of making a contribution to the discussion.

A variation on two of the approaches outlined here, the student paper and the whole group event, is the approach developed by Nisbet. Each student undertakes, within his chosen topic, to produce 'six statements worth making'. Each statement consists of a single sentence. The group's task, which spans two sessions, is, through questioning and discussion, to arrive at six formulations of the original statements that reflect an acceptable compromise among the individual positions held by members of the group. The approach is described more fully in Part II of this chapter.

c.   *Responsibility for clarifying issues of assessment*

There should be occasions in small group meetings where students can try out ideas, can take some intellectual risks. If discussion is to be assessed, however, students may prefer to play safe. The shadow of assessment is likely to make the enquiry more teacher-oriented than it might if there were no assessment or if the rules for assessment were made clear to the students.

Assessment presents dilemmas. What is being assessed? Is it talk, and if so, is it quantity or quality of talk? Is assessment likely to increase talkativeness at the cost of thoughtfulness? Will the student who makes a rare but always well-considered contribution be penalised? Will assessment induce competitiveness rather than cooperativeness in discussion or group activity? And if the small group is seen as an interdependent learning situation, can individuals be graded without reference to the group as a whole — or to the performance of the seminar leader whose responsibility it is to facilitate learning? (Part II includes a seminar leader's scheme for assessing talk in seminars.)

One way out of the dilemma of assessing the thinking that goes on during the seminar — in so far as it is communicated in talk — is for the seminar leader to base her assessment on written work. Here the challenge is to set work that can reflect the way in which a student's understanding and judgement have been influenced by the exchanges that have taken place in the group. Instead, what often seems to happen is that the written assignment is a very individual and private piece of work which could have been prepared even if the seminar had not taken place. Such a criticism is probably more true of arts seminars than of science seminars where the assignment may well be to represent the insights gained from a group task of solving a problem or conducting an experiment.

What is most important, once again, is that the seminar leader is explicit and consistent about the mode of assessment, and is prepared to make known – and even to discuss – the criteria that are being used.

d.   Responsibility for time-keeping

It may seem pedantic or over-serious to suggest that watchfulness over time is one of the seminar leader's major responsibilities, but experience and observation suggest that there are important issues here.

It is conventionally the seminar leader who marks the start and end of sessions and it is easy for her to extend the session because *she* feels that things are going well (it may of course seem to the students that they are being 'kept in') or because she fails to notice the time. Students tend to wait to be released, and it can be sheer indulgence on the part of the seminar leader to keep a group, unless the group as a whole express the wish to stay and continue the work. The argument for making an issue of time is this: if the group feels that the time boundaries matter and are secure, members are likely to arrive on time and to complete their task within the time. It is interesting to note how often the pace of activity accelerates towards the end of a meeting as the need to accomplish something establishes itself. If the time-boundaries are slack, this phenomenon is unlikely to occur. The keeping of time is part of the contract between staff and students. Indeed, one of the themes of this book has been the importance of providing a reliable framework for this very demanding form of learning, and consistency about time-keeping, as well as about role, procedures and criteria of assessment are crucial factors in the building of such a framework.

e.   Responsibility for maintaining the spirit of small group work

The loosely-worded heading covers a range of rather pious and sober concerns that relate directly to the peculiar potential of small group work – the promotion of interactive, participatory learning. The seminar leader, ideally, will be interested in students' thinking, and skilful in encouraging and eliciting half-formed ideas (without, however, interrupting to complete a sentence for the student – who rarely comes back to complain that what the *seminar leader* said is not what *he* meant to say!). The seminar leader should take care to be scrupulously fair to persons and to ideas, and to be demonstrably ready to learn (a 'seeker' rather than a 'knower' to use Bruner's cunningly simple distinction). She might also give thought to issues of reward and punishment in relation to her own authority. For instance, is the student, in small group work, always looking to her for reinforcement? If she feels that she has a responsibility for encouraging the nervous or slow into taking heart, what does the fine line look like that distinguishes encouragement from reward? It may be, in fact, that the best reward a student can have in small group work is the certainty that he will be listened to and will be taken seriously, by his peers as well as by the seminar leader. And what is the seminar leader's responsibility in relation to the dominant student, the disruptive student, or even the nonchalant/indolent student – the small group 'squatter'? Is she to take disciplinary action and if so, on behalf of the group as a whole or in her own right as staff representative in the group – or should she encourage the *group* to accept responsibility for dealing with members who do not pull their weight or do not contribute to the common task?

All this may sound very self-conscious, especially to the seminar leader who is confident, spontaneous and extrovert and believes she has no problems in her seminars. But there are people who find teaching a struggle and who gain some assurance from the idea that teaching can by systematically worked at and improved:

'Teaching is an art, not a science. But a useful art, perhaps comparable to architecture. Artists are not born but made: they train and they continue to train themselves. To say that teaching is an art is intended here to emphasize that it is learnable in the way that arts are learnable, and related to inquiry and research as arts are related to inquiry and research.'
(Stenhouse, 1976, an internal, unpublished paper for the Centre for Applied Research in Education, University of East Anglia.)

4.   *Jointly led seminars*

The practice of joint seminars (where two members of faculty are present at each meeting) is unlikely to be widespread given the heavy demands it makes on staffing. However, in some departments there is a tradition of jointly led small group work and it may be worthwhile to set out some of the issues. The main differences are whether the two staff members represent complementary specialisms or merely different perspectives from within the same specialism, and whether their roles are differentiated – for instance, whether they are present on equal terms and with similar responsibilities or whether one acts as consultant while the other leads the session.

The argument for having two colleagues from the same subject area is likely to be the opportunity for exposing students to different viewpoints. I interviewed a seminar leader about this (the passage below is taken from my notes on the interview):

'He went on to explain why it was important to have two faculty in a seminar. He said that in this way students had two points of view. There were no text books on the topic in which he was lecturing and therefore nothing to which they could refer but research papers which they were not always able to read and which only gave one point of view. He said that what students heard in a lecture they believed implicitly and what they read in the paper was absolute gospel truth to them. He said students have to try to learn to question. In a seminar at least they heard his point of view and his colleague's, both of which were different.'

The rationale for using two seminar leaders is here expressed in terms of access to knowledge. A different rationale would see the two seminar leaders as engaged in academic debate and thereby providing models for the students of professional discourse in action. An additional advantage claimed for this approach is that the students find the debate between seminar leaders intellectually stimulating and motivating. The disadvantage is that for students the seminar can become a spectator sport, where they learn by observation rather than by participation.

An alternative approach is where the two seminar leaders work together primarily to share the difficult procedural responsibilities of managing the seminar and facilitating the active learning of the students. This approach has been developed in the USA for literature seminars attended by both young and mature students (The Great Books Program). The co-leaders work together on the basis of a shared understanding of the aims of the meetings and of the conventions which are to govern behaviour at the meetings. These conventions have been fully articulated in a manual for co-leaders; the 'rules' are fairly specific and serve to make each leader accountable to the other and, in so far as the ground rules for discussion are made available to the group, serve also to make the co-leaders accountable to the participants. The rules are also designed to diminish the possibility of competitiveness and conflict between the two leaders. The central conception is that the co-leaders act as backstops to each other in the difficult task of encouraging reflective discussion:

'The value of a Great Books discussion as an educational experience depends upon how well you and your co-leader carry out your function. Good discussion doesn't occur automatically whenever you gather fifteen people around a table. It takes interest, concentration, digging, discipline, and respect for others. You are there to direct discussion by introducing the basic questions, and to guide it by seeking answers to your basic questions. You are not there to tell participants what to think, but to keep them examining in relation to the book whatever question happens to be on the floor for discussion . . .'

'Flexibility and close listening are essential traits for a co-leader. Remember that each participant thinks more about his own responses than he does about the possible relationships among all responses. It is your job to help him make connections through your questions. As co-leaders, you should have continual overall awareness of what is going on, of how one response fits with the next. Sometimes – and it should be encouraged – participants will assume some of your functions. For example, they will challenge statements made by other participants. But in any Great Books discussion no one except the leaders will be concerned with every response and with the discussion as a whole. The development of the discussion is always your responsibility.' (The Great Books Foundation, 1971, pp. 79-80)

THE EVIDENCE

1.   *A contract designed by a seminar leader to contain the effects of his authority*

    Moral Philosophy
    (please read twice and note any obscurities)

During this term we shall be doing more than Moral Philosophy; we shall be conducting an exploratory experiment in small group learning.

I.   *Hypothesis*

Most small group work, as at present conducted in this School* (perhaps in the university as a whole), obstructs the intellectual independence of students and leads them to depend on the faculty leader. The faculty leader, in turn, finds intellectual and emotional security in using his authority and expertise to dominate the small group situation. Minor frustrations apart, this set-up satisfies both students and faculty; but it may be educationally disastrous.

II.   *Phenomena consistent with this hypothesis*

    (1)   The faculty leader introduces, imposes and forces discussion back to *his own agenda*:

(a)   he takes note and pursues only those student remarks which can be used for or bent towards *his* ends;

(b)   his questions often have, as their only point, the eliciting of an already anticipated answer (for instance, they seldom express genuine puzzlement);

(c)   tensions arise when the expressed purpose of the small group (free discussion) clashes with the faculty leader's hidden agenda.

    (2)   In the shadows of the leader's agenda (either explicit or hidden), the students:

(a)   spend much energy in trying to guess at the leader's agenda (the guessing game);

(b)   try to get the leader to produce his agenda in a series of mini-lectures;

(c)   are reticent in producing remarks which cannot clearly be seen to fit the supposed agenda;

---

*School, i.e. Department of the University

(d)   direct all or most of their attention to the leader's remarks and little to those of each other (particularly true of the brighter student);

(e)   get many of their psychological rewards from anticipating or fitting their remarks to what they take to be the *leader's* goal. Punishments accrue insofar as they fail in this task.

(3)   Many students do not feel the intellectual or social need to prepare for small group work. They can be assured that the faculty leader will take the burdens of keeping things going:

(a)   watch for the use, by students, of the weapon of silence; and for the faculty leader's response:

(b)   notice how preparation for small-group meetings tails off when students realize that the *leader* will ensure that the relevant arguments, the important theses, the critical appraisals are covered *regardless of the volume and relevance of student contributions.*

III.   *Towards an alternative method*

If the hypothesis under I is correct, then there should be some arrangements which help small-groups to break the stranglehold of the faculty leader and generate some intellectual autonomy amongst students. The following strategies are directed to that end and they constitute the explicit conventions under which we shall work this term.

(1)   *Coverage of material:*

With the institution of examinations in the background, it is inevitable that students should worry about covering the ground. If this worry is taken into small groups then it is my impression that discussion can suffer; both students and faculty regard the small group as a means to extending coverage, consolidating information, reinforcing lectures. The leader enters the room with an agenda to be forced through, and the students attend with note-pads at the ready. To combat the demon of coverage, we shall test the following moves:

(a)   small group discussions will not be geared to the subject matter of preceding lectures

(b)   coverage of material will be achieved by a set of nine or ten lectures (Monday of each week), arranged to deal chronologically with moral philosophy from J.S. Mill up to the present time

(c)   each student will be required to take one of the following texts and study it in depth — hopefully, in cooperation with one or two other students. An essay will be written on this chosen text or on some aspect of it.

(List of several introductory texts)

(2)   *'Follow-up' lectures:*

At the *end* of each week, the course is timetabled for a second lecture. This is designed to allow me to *follow up* questions and issues raised by the small group meetings of the week. If there is nothing worth following up, or if we decide to use the hour differently, then the lecture will not be given. This is the only lecture time explicitly associated with the small group discussion material; the *first* lecture of each week is *not* designed to provide grist for the small group meetings.

(3)   *Agenda for small group meetings:*

The agenda for each week's seminar meetings will lie in the hands of the students. Each group of twelve will divide in half and each sub-group of six will take it in turn to sort out the week's agenda. Each sub-group will need to meet together (and with me) in the week *before* their week of responsibility to warn the others of the reading required for the following week's meetings. I will try to ensure that the necessary directions for the following week are duplicated for all members – and, if possible, the necessary reading. In week two, the other half of Group A will repeat the process, thereby deciding the agenda for week three.

Two things worth stressing. Firstly, that the sub-groups *really are* free to choose any topic falling under the head of 'Moral Philosophy'; they may decide to extract themes, arguments and assumptions from the manifesto of the Gay Liberation Front, or they may prefer to chop up an article by A.J. Ayer. Secondly, by the end of about the fifth week everyone ought to be picking out *patterns of, and relationships between, various problems.* By that time each group ought to be in a position to *string together* small group discussions so that their results are cumulative and connected.

(4)   *Conduct of small group meetings:*

It would be a mistake to think that small group meetings run on a student agenda are likely to be more informal or more comfortable. It will be an explicit convention that the sub group in charge of the week's meetings *does not present a sub group lecture to the other members;* the object of the exercise is that *everyone* should be prepared to contribute to the topic in question. The sub group which has decided the agenda is obviously in a better postion to *guide and help* the discussion, but its members have no more obligation to contribute than anyone else. At all costs we must avoid the phenomenon of a passive audience sitting through a class paper.

(5)   *Recessive faculty:*

It should be clear that our small group meetings are explicitly designed for *student-*

control; my own role will be recessive and consultative. As the groups (hopefully) gain internal solidarity it will be easier for me to enter the discussions without fouling up the pattern. Most of my time in seminars will be spent trying to identify the emerging themes and arguments of the discussion so that I can write them up for the second lecture of the week; any questions I ask should be requests for clarification.

(6)   *Assessment:*

It is important to make explicit that *nothing you do (or fail to do) in the small-group meetings will be assessed for grading purposes.* Grades for the course will be determined by two essays.

(a)   An essay on some one text, part or aspect of a text, chosen from the list under (1) (c). Due in: week 6

(b)   An essay on the title "Why should I be moral?" (Reading list to follow) If you wish to choose some other title then please see me first. Due in: week 9.

Although grades will be determined by the above essays, *no grade will be given unless you keep, week by week, a record of the work done for and in the small-group meetings.* This record will consist of a loose-leaf folder (35p at the Bookshop) containing:

Accounts of your work in the sub-group.

Accounts of the themes and arguments raised each week in the small group meetings

Three summaries of your own developing views, to be written at the end of weeks 3, 6 and 9.

These folders must be *given in at the end of the course* and, in addition, I will try to collect a few each week (from week 2 onwards) to comment on. (They will, of course, be returned the following term after the final collection.)

(7)   *Assessment of the course:*

We shall need to meet periodically to discuss what is going wrong and how we might put it right. I will try to arrange such sessions in weeks 3, 5 and 7. If any individual student has problems, then I am available at any time to discuss them — timetable permitting.

2.   *Other 'contracts' or programmes where attention is given to the roles and responsibilities of the seminar leader and students*

a.   *For a course on the poetry of T.S. Eliot for final year students*

Objects of the course

1.   To 'understand' some of Eliot's poems in detail, i.e. to make sense of some texts locally and in detail, and to internalise that meaning in relation to one's own life and perhaps also to the class. To be achieved mainly via the seminars.

2.   To acquire some grasp of Eliot as a whole – e.g. how his poems relate to plays or criticism, what themes or images recur. Mainly via lectures and written work. This objective might extend to literary and social context.

3.   To exercise the skills of articulation (of understanding, description, criticism, response etc.) orally and in writing (or in other visual modes); and of research (acquiring information, testing relevance etc.). It is in the exercise of these skills that class and private work unite.

Written work

Deadline 5 pm Friday 1 June (i.e. one week after end of course).

1.   An introduction to T.S. Eliot, consisting of a series of essays, chapters, etc., at least one by each member of the class; but the introduction is to be put together by the class as a whole, and one member's written work is to consist of being its editor, and writing an introduction to the volume.

2.   A series of exemplary pieces of brief local editing of selected parts of texts, such as we have already discussed in the class.

Grading: I shall give each individual a mark for the essay and the piece of editing that he does, together. I shall not count towards assessment anything that is said or done in the class.

Methods

Putting together the list of objectives and the written work, the methods are clear: that in class we work together towards highly local understanding, which then gets written up individually as 'editing' of those localities. We aim at wider grasp by means of the introductory essays, which are done individually but with class organisation. Obviously the quality of the final essays and pieces of editing will depend to some extend on the group as well as on the individual.

Roles

The tutor's roles in this seminar are:

(a)   To act as the boundary keeper, the person who attends to the relationship between the class and space, time, the university; perhaps also the boundary between people as members of the class and as private persons.

(b)   To act as a consultant to the work of the class.

The students' roles in this seminar are:

(a)   To act as consultants to the work of the class.

(b)   To be members of the class.

(c)   To pursue, or test, the objectives.

Resources available

The resources available to the students are: names of the whole class in writing; reading-list; assignment of preliminary exercises; statement of objectives, methods, roles, and written work; books on loan from the seminar leader; the university library (numerous books on short-term loan); texts in the hand; blackboard; four lectures (two with typescript quotations, one with a recording of Eliot reading his own poetry); various xeroxes including two of the facsimile of the MS of *The Waste Land*.

b.   *For a course on Modernism and Cultural Crisis for second and third year students*

1.   Here is a list of all the people participating in the session.
       (Note: the names were listed here.)

2.   Before next term, I want to make it quite clear that *I intend to run this seminar as a seminar.*

       That is to say:

(a)   I do not intend to deliver a series of mini-lectures.

(b)   I do not intend to take sole responsibility for the conduct of the group.

(c) If you come unprepared and do not talk in the seminar, I shall simply allow it to fall to pieces.

(d) I do not intend to fill in silences by frantic cover-up talk.

(e) *You* must take responsibility *with me* for making the seminar work: if you do not play your part, I shall not play mine.

(f) We shall sit round in a circle with the tables removed.

You have been warned!

3.   Work requirements:

(a) Two essays from each participant on whatever aspects of Modernism interest you.

(b) The first of these essays must be handed in by 12 noon on Friday of the fifth week of term. Late work will *only* be accepted if it is accompanied by a medical certificate or if you have seen me before the deadline to explain what is happening.

(c) The second of these must be handed in by 12 noon on Friday of the tenth week of term. The School* Regulations do not permit me to accept work after this dead-line without a valid medical certificate.

(d) My procedure for setting essays is as follows: you come and see me and tell me the general topic on which you want to write and I will tailor-make an essay title for you.

(e) Before each meeting of the seminar as a whole, a small, nuclear supervision-group will meet and go over the ground. Attendance at these sessions is *not optional* and absence from them will be penalized when I come to work out your final mark. It is also to your benefit to attend these supervision-groups. Students often complain that they do not get enough individualized attention — well, here is an opportunity to get a bit more.

4.   The aim of the seminar:

To give you some idea as to the meaning of Modernism, to analyze the nature of the cultural crisis experienced in Western Europe in the C20th, and to identify some of the responses to this crisis situation.

---

*School, i.e. Department, of the University

It is a seminar which requires intensive thought rather than extensive reading — though I won't, of course, object to your doing the latter as well as undertaking the former.

5.   Reading matter:

I shall provide wodges of duplicated matter. Many of the other books on the reading-list are on restricted loan and should be consulted in the library.

6.   Supervision-groups:

(18 groups of 3 students each — each student's name appearing in 3 groups — were listed. Students were told that dates and times of the meetings would be posted early next term. The meetings were to take place in the faculty common room.)

7.   Finally, I apologise for the categorical way in which I have set out the seminar requirements. I have done it like this for the following reasons:

(a)   So that I can keep off your backs next term. I do not intend to keep repeating what I have said here.

(b)   So that you know exactly where you are. A structure has been set up in which we will all work.

(c)   Because there seems to be general misapprehension about the nature of seminars and the conventions according to which they operate.

(d)   Because it has become clear to me that if we want seminars to work, then we have to work at making them work.

c.   *For an intensive two-week seminar, for mature students, in educational innovation*

Roles, responsibilities and resources

The *aim* of the two week course is to arrive at an identification and understanding of the issues that seem to be important in the dissemination and implementation of curriculum innovation.

Each member of the group is a *resource* in so far as he or she considers past experience relevant. I see it as my responsibility to offer my own experience as data and therefore to act as a resource on the same basis as other members of the group. I also see it as my responsibility to provide additional data to support the group in its study and to ensure that there is common ground as the basis for group discussion.

I see it as my *responsibility* to offer a structure for the two weeks of study. Emphasis and sequence (apart from the obvious fixed points of visiting speakers) are open to negotiation. I see it as the group's responsibility, within the proposed framework, to organise its way of studying and sharing insights in relation to the resources availabe, in relation to the time constraints and in relation to the task.

I shall try to maintain a distinction between my *role* as *contributor* (for instance, in giving an introductory talk, in making available my experience as the person in charge of the dissemination of the innovation being studied) and my *role* as *chairman* (on occasions where the group meets as a whole to discuss or report back).

3.   *Final year students comment on the use of the seminar paper*

'If the seminar leader, instead of saying to somebody "Well, you do the seminar paper on the book" had given them a definite theme — people can come to the seminar with an idea. Just general guide-lines so that you can think about it for 5 to 10 minutes before. People don't know what he's going to say until he actually says it.'

'They (seminar papers) are often very difficult to follow if they're written out as essays. Perhaps the person writing the essay is intent on writing a good essay and getting a good mark. He doesn't always give it as a very stimulating . . . sometimes he starts off and you just write a letter or something because you just can't follow it. If one just felt we were all thinking about the same sort of things, that would help, whereas when someone is giving a very close-woven class paper it assumes that they've got all the answers anyway — but the seminar is supposed to spark off the questions.'

'(I don't like) the system of a class paper being given a mark, assessed as an essay, in fact. Some people hand class papers in after they've written them. Just hand them straight in. They've written an essay out and they just read it. As to other people, their class papers can be quite different from the ones they write because they're prepared to learn and listen. In which case you can afford to have it much more provocative — but it doesn't always work. Sometimes they (the students) accept it. They don't realise you're trying to stimulate an argument. They write it all down.'

'If someone arrives with a class paper and says "I haven't found the answers yet" it turns out to be a much better seminar.'

'They (seminar papers) seem to be a lot more successful as far as the seminar discussion goes if the person who gives the paper isn't so definite, so fixed in their views. Some of the best seminars we've had are when people have come along and asked questions, posed questions for the seminar and the seminar tried to answer them.'

4.   *A variation on the seminar paper as the basis for discussion*

(The extracts are from an article by Nisbet, 1966.)

The students involved are graduate teachers attending an advanced class in *Theory of Education,* an obligatory class in the later stages of the work for our postgraduate degree in Education. Most of them are part-time students, coming to classes after school hours. Their average age is about twenty-seven. They have already had some professional experience and have already attended other courses in various branches of education and psychology . . .

The course in *Theory of Education* consists of two 1-hour lectures and a 1½-hour seminar meeting each week for one academic year. It is with the seminar meetings — about twenty-three in the year — that this article is concerned.

Each seminar group has eight students and a tutor. The whole subject of study is divided into about ten fields or areas — enough to allot one to each student and have one or two left over. (The current list of fields is as follows: Curriculum; Examinations; Methods; Discipline, including character-building and moral education; Administration; Finance; The Teacher; How Useful is Psychology?; How Useful is Sociology?; Educational Values.)

At the first meeting the tutor presents the list of fields, announces that each student is to choose one of these as the area within which he will make his major contribution, and asks them to indicate their individual preferences. Since there are a few more fields than students it is usually possible for each student to find a reasonably congenial field. The tutor explains that each student will be given two successive meetings of the seminar in which to make his contribution and so the programme for the first seventeen meetings is drawn up, thus:

> Meeting 1: Introductory
> Meeting 2: Curriculum 1 — Mr. A.B. Smith
> Meeting 3: Curriculum 11 — Mr. A.B. Smith
> Meeting 4: Examinations 1 — Miss C.D. Jones
> Meeting 5: Examinations II — Miss C.D. Jones
> Meeting 6: Methods 1 — Mr. E.F. Robinson
> Meeting 7: Methods 11 — Mr. E.F. Robinson

and so on to Meeting 17.

The tutor now expounds the procedure. Within each field the student responsible must first produce SIX STATEMENTS WORTH MAKING. What this involves has to be clearly understood: a 'statement worth making' (worth making, that is, in the context of this seminar) is one which is clear, succinct and important; which is controversial enough to require careful decision before it is accepted or rejected, and which represents the personal belief, based on study, experience and reflection, of its author. To put it negatively, statements not worth making are high-sounding platitudes, trivialities, vague abstractions whose acceptance or rejection would make no observable difference in practice, disingenuous 'O.K.' phrases, inadequately grounded opinions, or assertions that no one is likely to dispute. Each statement must consist of only a single sentence but the author will in due course be given every opportunity of providing supplementary details and explaining why he chose to formulate each statement in its present form. No attempt must be made to 'cover' the whole field; each statement can be as general or as specific as the author wishes, and the six chosen are to be regarded as a selection from the hundreds he could presumably produce in the given area of study if called upon to do so. When a student has made up his list he is expected to provide enough copies (with recommended references to relevant literature appended) to go round the group.

Meeting 2 begins with the circulation of the copies of Mr. Smith's statements on 'Curriculum' and a talk by Mr. Smith, preferably not longer than twenty minutes, to introduce them. The remainder of the meeting is devoted to free and informal discussion. The members of the group, including the tutor, ask Mr. Smith what he means by this and that, add their own observations, and even digress if they feel like it. Spontaneity and freedom are the characteristics of this meeting.

At meeting 3 Mr. Smith's statements are given their 'second reading'. Now the atmosphere is one of discipline, discussion and urgency, in contrast to the spontaneity and freedom of the previous discussion. Mr. Smith briefly reminds the group of what he considers the significant points made at the previous meeting and may even report a few second thoughts of his own in the form of amendments to the list of statements. Thereafter Mr. Smith has to take the group systematically through the list, trying to obtain unanimous agreement for each statement in turn. Whenever this is not immediately forthcoming (it hardly ever is: the statement would probably not be worth much if it was) he and the other group members, including the tutor, suggest amendments which might (a) satisfy the critics and yet (b) retain the support of those who approve the statement as it is and (c) still leave 'a statement worth making'. If after long discussion a compromise proves impossible the dissident member(s) will be left to compose a 'minority view' on the statement in question. All this is strenuous work, for the issues involve decisions on controversial matters and each member of the group, including the tutor, knows

that when the list is promulgated in its final form his name will appear as
one of its supporters. Members therefore strive to assist in the birth of group
formulations without doing violence to their own principles. Decisions, moreover, have to be made without undue delay. Almost invariably we find that
time is running short towards the end of a 'second reading' and a concent-
rated effort is necessary to produce acceptable versions expeditiously (the
tutor works particularly hard at this stage). When the time is up, however,
if it is felt that it has been quite impossible to do justice to a statement,
that statement is simply deleted from the list, the members being thus
absolved from committing themselves either to agreement or to disagreement.

At the end of this meeting Mr. Smith takes home the group minute book to
write up the official account of the two meetings for which he has been
responsible. Before the members finally disperse, however, Miss Jones, who
is to take the lead at the next two meetings, hands round advance copies of
the six statements (with references) which she is going to submit.

Meeting 4 opens with the reading by Mr. Smith of the official minute of
meetings 2 and 3. This minute consists of (a) the original list of statements;
(b) a very brief mention of the most prominent issues in the discussion; (c)
the list as finally agreed, with the names of members of the group (including
the tutor) who subscribed to it; and (d) 'minority views', if any, with the
names of members (again the tutor may be included) who uphold them. The
reading and approval of this minute (we usually take (a) as read and ask the
reader to start at (b)) should not occupy more than about ten minutes.

Miss Jones now takes over and introduces the 'first reading' of her statements (which, it will be remembered, the group has had a week to think
about). The same procedure is followed as with Mr. Smith's 'first reading',
the discussion being relatively free and unrestrained . . .

The method has been described exactly as I am at present using it, though
there is of course nothing sacrosanct about any of the details. As it stands,
however, it would seem to have the following advantages:

1.   The students are impelled to prepare carefully for each discussion
session. The selection, composition and justification of six 'worthwhile' statements involves much reading, thought and judgement on the part of the pres-
enter of the statements. This becomes abundantly clear after the first few
meetings, when the group has had the chastening experience of seeing several
plausible statements collapsing under cross-examination. The other members
of the group, too, are at least urged to do some preliminary reading and thinking, since they are given references along with the statements a week in advance.

2.   Theory and practice, fact and value, the desirable and the practicable,

the personal and the professional are all taken into account, since decisions have to be taken on real questions.

3.   The alternation of free and disciplined discussion periods allows the group to get the benefits of both — on the one hand the expansive, 'divergent' atmosphere of free talk, favourable to the evolution of new ideas and new outlooks, and on the other hand the salutary experience of a 'convergent' session at which a number of decisions must be made in a limited time, longwindedness and irrelevance being ruthlessly suppressed.

4.   The method makes it easy for the tutor to sustain his rightful role as primus inter pares — 'primus', in that he is chairman of the group, in so far as there is a chairman, and is responsible for the conduct of the meetings, occasionally supplying factual information, tactfully bringing in the less vocal members, keeping an eye on the clock, and exercising self-restraint by remaining silent when necessary, even at times when he would like to say a lot; 'inter pares', because he participates in the discussions on a footing of equality, criticizing and being criticized, asking and answering, revealing his own personal values as well as exploring those of the students.

5.   The procedure, once grasped, is simple. After the first meeting it is virtually self-regulating and requires little or no administration by the tutor until the programme for the concluding meeting has to be arranged.

6.   One might even claim a vocational benefit. Professional people must be able to play their part effectively on committees, boards, councils and the like. What could be more relevant to this than practice in giving shape to a consensus of opinions, in respecting the views of others as well as one's own, and in tactfully probing apparently irreconcilable positions to see how much of the antagonism is real, how much emotion, and how much semantic? An effective member of a committee is patient, tolerant, constructive, able equally to lead and to follow as occasion demands, willing to take the trouble to inform himself about facts, and skilled in the art of creative compromise. Such qualities are fostered, or at least encouraged, in the seminars I have described.

7.   Lastly it may not be out of place to remark that seminars of this sort are stimulating and beneficial to the tutor as well as to the students. Every group is completely different from every other group. Every meeting is a unique occasion, with new confrontations, new patterns of thought, new personal encounters and new constructive opportunities, In fact, the task of conducting such seminars as these is one which becomes more absorbing as the years go by.

(This edited version of Professor Nisbet's paper, which was prepared by the author, was reproduced, with permission, in *Small Group Teaching: selected papers*, a compilation by the Nuffield Foundation's Group for Research and Innovation in Higher Education.)

5.   *Assessing oral contributions in seminars: a proposal*
(An internal university paper by Dr. Holger Klein prepared for discussion at a Board of Studies meeting.)

A.   Prefatory remarks

The comments I received on my plea to allow oral work to carry up to 20% of the grade in a seminar have so far been discouraging. Nevertheless I feel bound to put before the members of the Board my arguments on what I believe to be an issue of great importance.

I should like to mention that in the face of nearly unanimous rejection of my proposals I shall not at present bother the Board with a formal motion but shall *nolens volens* conform to the long-standing practice of the School.

In view of this a perusal of what follows is recommended only to those colleagues who are not absolutely convinced that the point is not worth considering.

B.   Nature of the proposal

I   Oral contributions to the work of a seminar group must be assigned a definite weight in each seminar grade.

II   The weight actually given to oral work may vary to suit the varying character of different seminars.

III   It should, however, represent a minimum of 5% and should not exceed 20%. Taking the figures of 5, 10 15 and 20% not only will facilitate an already simple calculation but also has the additional advantage that these portions can be more easily visualized than, say, 7 or 13%.

IV   It seems extremely difficult to me to say that a piece of written work deserves, e.g., 57 instead of 54. It is obviously more difficult to do the same with a student's oral contributions. A simpler scale of 10 classes mounting by multiples of 10 is less problematic and more workable.

V   The result is a slight downgrading of students who contribute little or nothing to the group's joint effort and a slight positive adjustment of the grade of students who do.

C.   Examples

The following examples show the effect of the proposed system on the grade with varying ratios of weight assigned to written and oral work.

I   Model calculation: Mark given to witten work: 37 (out of 100)
                          Mark given to oral work: 50 (out of 100)

Ratio	Calculation	Aggregate Mark
95:5	$\dfrac{(37 \times 95) + (50 \times 5)}{100}$	37.65
90:10	$\dfrac{(37 \times 90) + (50 \times 10)}{100}$	38.30
85:15	$\dfrac{(37 \times 85) + (50 \times 15)}{100}$	38.95
80:20	$\dfrac{(37 \times 80) + (50 \times 20)}{100}$	39.60

II   Other examples (applying the same type of calculation)

Separate Marks WW:73/ /OW:40		Separate Marks WW: 65/ /OW:100		Separate Marks WW:48/ /OW:20	
Ratio	Aggregate	Ratio	Aggregate	Ratio	Aggregate
95:05	71:35	95:05	66.75	95:05	46.60
90:10	69.70	90:10	68.50	90:10	45.20
85:15	68.05	85:15	70.25	85:15	43.80
80:20	66.40	80:20	72.00	80:20	42.40

III   Rounding off

There are several standard procedures, I understand. One could ignore all decimal points; one could round up everything above and including .5, or one could round up the second decimal point above and including 5 to the first decimal. I leave the decision of what would be best in this case to experts.

D.   'Oral Work' specified

I   Under the heading 'oral work' different kinds of contribution may be mentioned. I can think of four main categories:

1) Contributions to a discussion on a previously announced topic
2) Impromptu contributions in a discussion which was not planned
3) Autonomous introduction by a coherent contribution of a topic not introduced by the seminar leader
4) An oral contribution of some length assigned by the seminar leader.

3) can be invited, but relies on the initiative of the individual; 2) is very much a question of the individual's temperament but is, from whatever point one considers it, 'a good thing'; 1) I regard as an important element of seminar work, 4) as well; both can be expected of a student and will help him towards adequate oral expression of his thoughts.

II   Example

'For next Thursday, please look closely at Sonnet 18 and these two translations of it so that in our discussion of them we may arrive at an appreciation of their relative merit and also at a better understanding of the sonnet itself.'

1) Students A-E do this and have something to say; student F, it turns out, has not looked at them; students G and H not only 'have something to say' but bring up important points which help the group's work as a whole.

2) The discussion expands into a consideration of the question: 'Can poetry be translated, should it be' etc. F talks a great deal, of which only a small amount is useful. A-D contribute little, E nothing, nor does H. G is consistently good.

3) E tries to get the discussion back to Sonnet 18 and finally succeeds. He has found another translation and points out its merits.

4) B had been assigned the task of summarizing some critical comments on Sonnet 18. He has seen four and acquits himself with moderate success. To queries he has only the answer of this or that critic but has not formed an opinion of his own.

5) G and H add further points, A is now more active. F points out the apparent inconsistency of 'May-Summer' and is crushed by G and B.

III   This is only one example, and one could hardly give marks for oral work on this basis. However the four main types of oral contribution are demonstrated by it and, I think, ways of assessing them have become visible.

If all students are assigned a task of category 4) more than once and if 1) is used several times, one can, from these two alone, arrive at a fairly adequate notion. If, in addition, a brief note on the performance under 2) is jotted down and eventual 3) entries are kept, the classification of the students' oral work in one of 10 groups should present no more difficulty than deciding on their written work.

E.   Argument

    I   Main Points

        1)   A system of university courses which have seminar teaching as their backbone is greatly to be welcomed.

        2)   Its main advantage as compared to a system which primarily relies on lectures and single tutorials is the possibility of discussion, of a live (and hopefully lively) multilateral exchange of ideas and information and of the interaction of personalities.

        3)   It implicitly expresses a belief in the value of discussion, in the possibility that students may also learn from one another.

        4)   Counting written work only in the assessment of a student's performance is inconsistent with the seminar system as such. It suddenly declares all discussion as void of significance and reduces the system to something like a correspondence course, or at best, a "University of the Air".

        5)   If most students were not interested in the subject and at the same time good-natured, they would take their cue from the present system's avowal that the soul of seminar work, discussion, is, after all, not to be taken seriously, and there would be little or no discussion, as there is no reward.

        6)   As most students, however, are good-natured and as many do, in fact, go to considerable trouble in preparing for sessions, it would not only seem just – even if the beliefs outlined above were not shared – to award them a certain amount of credit for it (a *certain* amount!). And for the same reason, it would seem nothing but equitable that a pointed failure to contribute to the joint effort of the group were reflected in a limited downgrading of the mark.

    II   Objections

        1)   Subjective Errors

There is room for subjective error in all kinds of assessment. That of oral work does not seem to contain more than any other. Written work, may, e.g., not have been written at all by the person whose name it bears; or it may in part contain unacknowledged debts to critics the teacher happens not to have read; or it may reproduce very pleasingly thoughts the teacher intimated in the seminar and is (unconsciously maybe) delighted to find again. At least the first possibility is much less likely to occur in oral work.

There is the objection that oral contributions are fugitive and cannot be reconsidered. This is a real point, but it can be considerably alleviated by procedures such as outlined in D, III.

There is, lastly, the point that oral work can only be judged by the teacher of the seminar and that means, usually, by only one person. However, the scope of what I propose must be considered here. If a colleague is not to be entrusted with taking one fifth of the grade as his personal responsibility in this field, then this sad state of affairs ought to apply to all fields; one would have to demand, e.g., that not only borderline-papers but all papers produced for course work be read by at least two different people.

2)   Pressure

I have been told that taking oral work definitely into account would constitute undue pressure on the students. To this I can only reply, that there is a great deal of pressure in written work as well. Moreover, as oral work is spread out much more, its pressure effect is much smaller. This line of argument, incidentally, was the driving force behind all cases I have heard made out for taking into account course work in general as well as examinations.

3)   Individual temperaments

People have told me that the system I propose would be unjust to students who are shy and self-conscious and who for this reason will not say anything or at any rate very little in class. I know this type of student very well — I belonged to it. And unfortunately I was taught in groups of between 30 and 200 members where there was no chance of a remedy.

Given the smaller numbers in our seminars here, I would argue that shyness which prevents a student from talking in such a group ought not to be left alone but ought to be diminished —

it will represent a major disadvantage to the person concerned in whatever career he or she may embark upon later. By assigning tasks like the one mentioned under D, I, 4) and by making D, I, 1) a matter of habit, one will get enough out of a student to assess him orally. By creating a relaxed atmosphere and by infusing confidence in the student through his performance of definite tasks, one will also indirectly encourage contributions in categories 2) and 3).

Conversely, the type of student who talks a great deal of rubbish was held up to me. Surely we can distinguish between solid and flimsy stuff when we hear it just as well as when we see it. There is only one important difference: when we see it, it is usually too late to suggest improvement.

F.   Conclusion

I   There are other arguments, but these I think are the principal ones. If they fail to convince, the others will too.

II   By proposing a range of weight of oral work of between 5 to 20% I act a little against my conviction which would favour the range of 15 to 20%. But as my proposal stands, it will, I hope,

1)   Accord some sort of credit for an important part of the students' work.

2)   Allow individual teachers to allot those weights to the students' different efforts which they think appropriate with regard to any particular seminar.

3)   Improve the standard of preparation for seminar sessions and thus exert a positive influence on them.

4)   Encourage thought and experiment in that vital field of teaching, assessment, and, as a corollary, in the methods of teaching themselves.

CHAPTER IV   PRACTICAL MATTERS

THE ISSUES

Seminars at different universities and colleges invariably reflect in some way the shadow of the institution – whether its policy, academic values, or just its architecture. Factors like group size, length of sessions, life-span of a seminar group, aspect and furnishings of seminar rooms, methods of enrolment for seminars – all these things are likely to influence the seminar leader's management of the seminar and students' opportunities for participation. If they are not entirely within the control of the seminar leader, they may at least lie within her realm of influence.

1.   *A matter of group size*

What is the ideal size for a student discussion group? The question is often asked, and in a way that implies that research workers should have come up with a definitive answer by now! But the question is more of a riddle than that. Answers from research are likely to be so hedged round with qualification that one does just as well to explore the folk-lore of experienced teachers and students.

In secondary education, discussions are not uncommonly attempted in groups of between twenty and thirty students, but teachers (working on the discussion approach developed by the Humanities Curriculum Project) have reported that with group sizes of sixteen to twenty-five pupils, discussion tends readily to turn into argument – so fragile is the tradition of discussion in our schools compared with the tradition of debate. The argument is shaped by a few dominant voices, pupils take sides, and cooperative learning gives way to competitive display:

'I like a good argument. I like to have somebody on the other side of the table who, you know, if he's got a belief, like, you know, trying to turn them . . . I like to have the facts on my side to put his wrong.'
(Fourth year pupil comments on 'discussion')

Teachers working with adolescents have also reported that a group size of five or six pupils is too small: there tends not to be sufficient diversity of perspective to open up the exploration of issues and the peer group pressure may not be strong enough to control a dominant and disruptive pupil (the assumption, here, is that in discussion work the teacher-chairman will jettision conventional authoritarian ways of disciplining pupils).

In higher education, however, seminar leaders and students whom I have interviewed prefer a group of between six and ten members. Problems arise in a small group, as in the adolescent group, if there is no diversity of experience and style to bring vigour and surprise to the enquiry. It seems that it is easier for students to talk in a very small group — but more difficult for them to find the content which will support depth of learning.

The seminar leader may well find, however, that her Department may not provide her with groups that fall within the desired size range. She will then need to consider ways of breaking down an outsize group (see chapter VI) and of setting up, for a very small group of likeminded or recessive students, tasks that will lead to differences in outcome so that the members can talk from their own experience. In a large seminar group the problem remains of how many students a seminar leader can effectively monitor if a system of continuous assessment is being used.

2.   *A matter of group formation and group stability*

There are three questions worth asking:

a.   What can be said for and against the different ways of forming seminar groups — and is this procedure something that a department should be concerned about on the grounds that the way groups are formed is likely to affect behaviour within the group?

b.   How long does it take for a group to learn to work effectively together?

c.   What can be said for or against small group work which brings together students from different years?

These questions are explored below.

a.   It can be chastening to reflect on the implications of traditional procedures for forming small groups. Procedures commonly encountered include these:

– *groupings determined by staff*

Alphabetical: this approach is likely to strike students as impersonal and logical — possibly bureaucratic. One seminar leader was experiencing considerable frustration as a result of this procedure (which was the convention within a department whose students he was working with on a minor course). Overseas students formed a high proportion of the year group; many students had the same surname and many had language difficulties. The alphabetical procedure adopted within the organising department produced several small working groups of students of similar cultural background, and as a result, the seminar leader's newly developed programme of small group work, committed to cross-cultural learning as well as to the promotion of confidence in talking about science, was seriously constrained.

Notional quality: colleagues in Senior Common Room conversations have sometimes been heard to label groups of students as 'good' and 'poor', and the speakers have gone on to speculate whether a streaming principle should operate in small group work in order to produce homogeneous groups of high contributors and low contributors.* It is worthwhile in such contexts to recall that teacher expectations of student performance can radically affect the way that students perform and their level of achievement. (See Rosenthal and Jackson, 1968)

— groupings determined by students

Options/signing the list: where students are invited to opt for groups, it is interesting to consider, and even find out, what criteria they use — content? reputation of staff (what, incidentally, do students value in seminar leaders)? congenial peers? What constraints operate, and with what effects, in option systems where students sign for the seminar group they wish to join? If some groups are over-subscribed and some under-subscribed, by what means, if even-sized groups are to be achieved, are some students re-assigned? If a maximum size is stated in advance (often on a first sign, first served basis) some students will be working in a second-choice group — indeed a group might consist largely of students for whom this topic or this tutor might constitute a forced choice.

Given the general concern with student motivation, the effect on students' attitudes of different principles of group formation is probably worth reflecting on.

b.   Many small groups have a butterfly life. They form, work for a term, and fade. They may not meet for more than one hour a week, for nine weeks of a term, and in such a context it may be difficult to establish a working relationship that taps the intellectual potential of members of the group and helps them to engage productively with ideas. Groups need time to learn to work creatively together.

It seems that sometimes staff working with small groups of students make assumptions about students' knowing each other. It is possible, however, that in a subject year group of sixty students, where the composition of the group is determined by staff without reference to student choice or student friendship patterns, then only a minority of students in any one seminar group are likely to know each other well and to mix socially outside the working group. The opportunity for the group to continue its enquiry in non-timetabled situations is therefore limited. The life of a group equals the time spent in the seminar room.

c.   Some institutions encourage the formation of small groups of students of different years. The argument is likely to be that students with at least one year's experience of small group work can provide a model for inexperienced students and in fact manage an unselfconscious induction for them. Of course, it might also be said that there are areas where the skills or knowledge of the longer-

---

*See the report prepared by teachers at Homerton College of Education on the attitudes of high contributors and low contributors in small group discussions.

serving students could inhibit the novitiate − in short, the authority that is commonly invested in the teacher may well be diffused through the older or more experienced members of the group, and it may be just as difficult for the junior members to come to terms with.

3.   *A matter of time*

a.   There are advantages in having a block of time for small group work − particularly for small group work which is trying to do more than clarify issues raised in a lead-lecture. Blocks of time (i.e. at least two hours, ideally a morning) allow variations of pace within a single working session. It can be important to recognise that small group work at its intensive best (whether this is manifest as powerfully vocal and lively exchanges or as more reflective interaction) is not generally sustainable for very long; flat passages are likely to occur, periods when individuals switch off or when the group as a whole relaxes and recharges itself − when members mark time and engage in what can seem to the outsider like almost conspiratorial sequences of academic small talk. Then the next issue is identified and the involvement begins to build up again. These plateaux seem to be functional − and in longer-lasting seminars it becomes easier for the group to tolerate breathing spaces; in the short one-hour seminar a flat patch can seem a bad patch − and the flat patch can be more difficult to break out of if there is a keen sense of time lost. A common complaint is that the seminar has only just got going when it is time to wind it up.

b.   A block of time makes it more possible to vary the pace of activity − and the kind of activity (discussion, private reading, individual writing, peer group consultation in pairs or trios). It also makes it feasible to attempt a group task. By 'group task' we mean something that actively engages members of the group and where there is an identifiable product, for instance, the editing of a set of papers, the designing or testing of a model, making an audio-visual record of an event, writing a proposal for a project, and so on. A group task, time permitting, allows a group to identify and bring into play the individual talents of its members, and it provides a sense of purpose and a sense of achievement. Moreover, if a task spans several meetings, it guarantees a realistic continuity (one that is carried in the experience of students) rather than the usual and often illusory continuity that is created in the opening remarks of the seminar leader.

c.   It is interesting to see how often small group meetings are conceived as a sequence of self-contained units − programmes rarely seem to be designed and communicated in terms of five week or ten week spans. Where an extended task gives coherence and continuity to a sequence of meetings, the vicissitudes of individual meetings matter less − what is important is the *overall* achievement of the group. The extended task, then, emphasises continuity and collaboration as features of small group work, and it also makes possible a variety of pace and activity that, as has been suggested above, seems positively to affect the motivation and application of group members.

4.   *A matter of place*

Proust once said that the only true voyage would be not to travel through a
hundred different lands with the same pair of eyes but to see the same land
through a hundred different pairs of eyes. Small group work is about learning
through different pairs of eyes — and the most appropriate seating pattern is therefore one which allows face to face interaction among all the members.

Casual seating with individuals at different levels (i.e. some on the floor) and at
different distances from each other is likely to make participation more difficult
for some members. Casual seating sets up expectations of casual learning. A formal
arrangement of chairs — a circle, arc or square — seems more appropriate. Chairs
without tables can seem threatening to students who are unused to working in
small groups. The table provides security as well as a resting place for papers. A
recessive or alienated student may communicate his feelings by withdrawing his
chair from the formal pattern; such a move seems more difficult when chairs are
set round a block of tables.

When chairs are arranged in an arc (often because the group will, at some time, use
the blackboard or watch a video-tape monitor or closed-circuit television set), it
is advantageous for the seminar leader to sit at one extreme. If she sits one or two
places in, she may cut off the extreme students from the rest of the group. If she
sits at the apex, she provides an obvious focal point and can become a telephone
exchange for comments — or she may be seen to divide the group so that the two
sides act in opposition. At the edge of the arc, the seminar leader seems able to
exert procedural control when necessary and yet not get in the way of student-to-
student discussion.

In a circle or square, the position of strength is that immediately facing the seminar
leader (the magnet seat for the student who enjoys challenging the authority of
the leader). This direct confrontation position can also support collusion between
student and staff. An awkward position for a student is to be sandwiched between
the seminar leader and a dominant student, or one who is reading the seminar
paper. Students in this position have confessed to feeling as insignificant as the
net in a game of tennis.

To summarise then, it is unfortunate if the allocated working space with its arrangement of chairs does not

—   allow face to face interaction among all members of the group;

—   allow easy access to the blackboard for students as well as for the seminar
       leader;

—   make available surfaces for books and papers so that students can comfortably read and write during the seminar;

—   provide some pinboarding and shelving (even small portable shelves) where reference and resource material can be displayed or accommodated so that members of the group can contribute material and make use of it during the seminar.

If rooms appropriate for seminars are not easily available, an expedient (indeed sometimes a preference) is the use of the seminar leader's study as a seminar room. The obvious advantage of this is the accessibility of a wide range of reference material. But there are disadvantages for the students. The working space is the seminar leader's territory. The students are surrounded by her paraphernalia, her chair, books, telephone, ornaments — the marks of her knowledge, interest, style, reputation and achievement; in short the marks of her professional and personal identity and authority. Only the seminar leader can find her way to and through the resources. Having the seminar in the seminar leader's study may put students at a disadvantage.

Small group work in science teaching can pose particular problems. It seems that science blocks are not always equipped with seminar rooms that are suitable for discussion. A scientist who wishes to use a seminar room (as opposed to her own study) might have to book a room in another block. Movement can create problems: seminar rooms often have the bleak non-identity of chain-motel rooms. If they are to provide a working context in which the students feel at home, then the seminar leader may have to transport from some distance books, charts, papers, models. In order to prepare a working room which is located in another block, she would need to have free time in the session preceding the seminar.

Much of what has been said above may seem obvious. It is difficult to gauge both what can confidently be said and what is worth saying. Abercrombie points out the dilemma:

> 'The physical environment in which a group meets, the comportment of the teacher and the expectations of the students are very important in group teaching. They are not more influential than in conventional teaching situations, but there they are accepted, self-understood, so ritualized that people conform to them automatically and unquestioningly and in so doing ignore them. Undoubtedly with the rapid increase in the use of group methods, it will soon be unnecessary to spell out the factors that control group behaviour also. Currently, it is necessary to do so because in the present context of education the nuances of behaviour in groups are as little understood as are those of the actors in a Japanese opera by a Western audience.' (1971, p. 25)

5.   *A matter of resources*

Discussion here is restricted to one broad category of resources which would include items such as books, off-prints of articles, copies of extracts from books and other print sources, tapes, slides and simple models. These are the most commonly used resources across all disciplines or fields.

The problem most frequently cited by students and teachers is shortage of texts. The difficulties are, of course, most acute when members of parallel groups are engaged on a common topic. Teachers complain that students are reluctant to buy books; students complain that copies are insufficient to meet immediate needs. The implications for discussion are serious. Group discussions cannot be reflective and will lack substantial critical bite if they are not grounded in some common experience. They are likely to become a minority pastime, with two or three cognoscenti holding the floor and the unprepared members sitting back and taking notes. Or, there will be a take-over by the seminar leader, since instruction may be the only means of providing a common experience for the group to work on.

Despite the obviousness of the problem, alternatives seem not to have been widely tried out — possibly because of financial and organisational implications. One way through would be the provision of sets of seminar books, on the model of sets of plays which libraries stock for amateur dramatic work. The sets could be borrowed for a particular unit of small group study. Another approach might be through the preparation of multiple copies of dossiers of material on a given theme. Students would then have individual copies of key passages of text, context, and criticism which could be explored directly in discussion. A different strategy would be to encourage collaborative reading among members of the small group. Where there are six books to be read for the course, and limited copies, individuals or pairs might undertake to study one book and to prepare notes for other members of the group. There are two difficulties here: first, students may not be competent in reading, extracting and presenting concisely the issues that are essential for discussion. Note-taking for oneself and note-taking for others are tasks that require different approaches and different criteria; second, the strategy probably requires syndicate groupings — that is, sub-groups of students which work independently of the teacher, with the teacher acting as a convenor/coordinator and resource consultant. Another possibility is the audio-visual presentation of essential evidence (a scene from a play, an interview, units of instructional material).

It might be worth glancing at some tangential issues that the resource problem raises or reveals:

i.   Departmental or institutional arrangements for copying materials. Students and teachers often admit to uncertainty about departmental protocols for copying materials for small group work. Departmental provision varies considerably both within and between institutions. Budgets may need to be revised and systems and procedures more clearly communicated. The copyright issue may have to be faced if longish extracts are being copied in substantial quantities.

ii.   Competing pressures on students to read. It is easy to forget that students may be involved in more than one course in any term. There are competing demands on time. Preparation in areas where students know they may have to hunt their books before reading them is likely to take a low priority.

iii.   The book-list and small group discussion. Small group work relies on common ground within the group. The expectation may be that common ground will be achieved outside the seminar through preparatory private study. Book-lists that are very short can define the common ground but there are the hazards of book-borrowing and book-buying. A return to the traditional 'basic reader' might in fact be a prudent move if purchase were a prerequisite of joining the course. (The preparation could of course require inter-institutional cooperation.) Students complain of long, undifferentiated book-lists distributed at the start of the course. Teachers may be reluctant to ascribe reading priorities lest they are seen to be condoning a minimum effort. But the minimum, if it is a commonly achieved min-mum, is probably more productive for small group work than broad differences in the areas and amounts of preliminary study. It seems logical that *essential* evidence for discussion be available in multiple copies so that it can be met and examined by the group as a whole. The long, undifferentiated book-list then begins to make sense; it can support individual patterns of reading; lines of study are marked out by interest and experience rather than by teacher prescription – and there is less likelihood of all the students wanting exactly the same library copies at the same time.

iv.   Authority in relation to the provision of resources. There are subtle – as well as obvious – ways in which the scarcity of resources can reinforce the authority problem for the group. The mechanism is roughly the same in each case: knowledge – or the grounds for getting a critical grip on knowledge – is the possession of the teacher: she will control the use of evidence, and her criteria for selection may not be made explcit; she may share evidence in ways which will make it difficult for students to make a critical response. Some symptoms of the authority/resources problem are these:

—   The teacher brings into the seminar room a pile of reference books in single copies; the students have no reference books (probably only note books). Passages may be marked (i.e. there is evidence of pre-determination by the seminar leader). These extracts may be used in an acceptable way – for instance, to give support to minority views expressed in the group, or to extend the range of consideration in the group. But if the extracts are used exclusively to support the view being put by the seminar leader, the students are in the awkward position of having no authoritative extracts to strengthen their own positions.

– The teacher (or the student) may read aloud from the single copy sources. The reader is familiar with the text; the listeners are not. It is difficult to make a critical scrutiny of data that is carried by something as evanescent as spoken words. Where the content lends itself to some form of blackboard presentation, the seminar leader's contribution, caught in chalk, can be more readily subjected to critical appraisal by the students. However, the blackboard can reinforce the authority problem if the seminar leader has a monopoly on its use, and if she seats herself where she appears, to the group, as the guardian of the board.

– The only relevant second-order material available may be the work of the seminar leader herself. Teachers in new fields of study where the seminar is exploring a specialist topic and where there are no text books available have themselves alerted us to the difficulties. One resort is for the teacher to legitimise critical response by students to her own work; she may need to adopt a neutral chairing role which will prevent her from making impatient or defensive moves.

THE EVIDENCE

1. *Final year students comment*

I met, informally, six final year students and raised with them some of the issues that seemed to me to be important: group membership, group stability, seminar rooms, timing of seminars, group size. What follows is an edited version of the transcript of the discussion.

Membership of seminar groups

JR: Do you know how you get into the group that you're in?

5: Sometimes. (laughter)

JR: Can you say what the system is, if there is a system. There may not be.

5: It's self-selected. We're a (sub) group working on a project – that's self-selected . . . In others I've no idea how the group are selected.

2: Sometimes it seems to be alphabetical. They sometimes give out a sheet. It starts at 'A' and ends at 'Z' and they just make some sort of decision.

5: There was one that was really peculiar because it looked as though our group had been selected because we were all the voluble types but in fact it was just coincidence we'd been selected — it wasn't entirely alphabetical. It was a combination of alphabetical and what other courses you were doing, or something like that.

JR: But you actually started to speculate as to why you had got that group?

6:    It was really incredibly noticeable — there was one quiet person in a group of about twelve.

5:    And the lecturer made the suggestion that perhaps he should change around the seminar groups.

JR: What do you think about doing it alphabetically?

5:    You get an arbitrary seminar group that would have constancy whatever course you were doing — you would be in the same sort of seminar group.

JR: What principle would you recommend then?

2:    Well, one of the seminars I was sitting in on last term, it was really noticeable that there were about four people who had different angles on the problem. One was a historian of some type and another one was a, well, (pause) a fresh air freak of some kind. All these different types, they all put their different slant on the problems, so we were looking at the problems as a whole. If you all believe in the same thing it's very difficult to generate discussion.

1:    I guess that there are two ways of arranging a seminar — putting all the quiet ones together in the hope that someone will eventually say something — they're not going to be masked by the noisy ones. But having had an experience of that sort of situation in one of the seminars, there's not enough that ever comes up that's stimulating. You've got to put some sort of noisier or vocal people in. With ideas.

5:    What is the criterion of success? Is the criterion of success simply that you get everyone to speak? I can't imagine that it is.

.   .   .

JR: If you're a fairly stable group — I don't mean emotionally, I mean because you've worked together for quite a time — and you get seminar leaders coming in and out, it seems to me that the real strength and the power actually lies with you.

5:    Yes.

JR: Does it feel like that? Can you talk about that?

2:    In one of my courses where we had been in the same seminar group
for the whole of last term and this term, if we get a new seminar
leader — well we have about four seminar leaders, there's usually more
coherence between us as a group and the seminar leader is sort of out
on a limb and often he doesn't know as much about what we know
about each other — if you follow what I mean*. For example, we had
one seminar when we had a furious discussion and where everybody
got really worked up and the next week we had a different seminar
leader and he mentioned the same topic and of course we all burst
out laughing and he didn't know why. That's one aspect.

Seminar rooms

JR: Let's just shift for a moment on to seminar rooms. Are there any
general comments you can make about where to meet, or what's the
ideal seminar room?

4:    You've got to be facing each other. You've got to be in a position
where you can see virtually everybody else in the room. I've had one
or two where there are people with their backs to you and you feel a
bit uncomfortable if somebody is talking behind you.

JR: How do you get into a position where there are people in rows, or
where you are not facing?

3:    Well perhaps you walk into the room and it's almost a square but there
are a few tables and the thing starts and people come and they've got to
sit down somewhere and I think it just evolves that way. Perhaps the room
is a bit too small to start with and people are sitting on the edge.

---

*Note: a parallel group of final year students from a different School who had worked
together in the same seminar group for two years took up this issue and made some different
points:

'We've been together for four years and we know that B is always going to try "to
transcend reality"; C is always going to have quite a rational approach; J — nobody
ever knows what she's talking about.'

'It does have the disadvantage of knowing who is going to speak and just sort of
accepting it. It has the same pattern every time.'

'There are certain people you tend to answer or rather argue with. You know you're
likely to be provoked, or disagree, because you usually do. And the group waits for
these two people.'

'You do tend to know the level of thought. You can relate quickly to the level of
thought.'

5:    Most seminar leaders would try to get a circle but some might forget and accept that the seating is the way that you *want* to sit.

1:    It's better to have a room that's too small than too big because if you have a great big sort of circle of tables you tend to get your students grouped around the three sides and your seminar leader on the fourth and no one will go and sit next to him until there's nowhere else to sit. (laughter) Wherever he sits down to begin with people will sort of cluster on the other side of the room. If you've got a smaller room you sort of get pressurised into sitting by him.

4:    It makes a bit of an 'us' and 'them' situation.

5:    There are some quite deplorable seminar rooms, I think.

2:    Perhaps the seminar leader ought to come in last when everybody else has spaced themselves round.

JR: Any other observations on rooms?

5:    In the seminars on personal space, it was predicted that rooms without a view would contribute to poor results and where there was a view it wasn't found to be so, but my own personal liking is to have at least a decent sized window in a seminar room.

1:    I just find that a distraction.

5:    I find it takes the pressure off somewhat.

6:    Well, in the Arts block it doesn't because all you can see is sky or another bit of concrete. It doesn't seem to make any difference at all.

3:    I sit by a window in case I get bored. (laughter)

JR: Do you take things into seminar rooms? The thing that always strikes me is that you may be in it once a week but there's nothing of you about it and you suddenly have to start working in it, and thinking in a room that somehow doesn't signal support for thinking.

5:    I'm not conscious of any sense of loss; in fact I think if you did have things in that room, that could well – far more than a window – be a source of distraction.

JR: So you accept the notion that you just go in and you just start spinning ideas?

3:   Well the seminar leader will already represent that to you, won't he? He's been lecturing to you during the year, so when he comes in you feel 'Well, now, this is our group, this is our subject', so it does feel right.

.   .   .

JR: Do you ever have a seminar in your tutor's study? Does this happen?

3:   We did have it. It was simply because there were only five or six of us anyway and we could fit in.

JR: Do you have any comments on that particular experience? Or on that situation in general?

5:   I've a feeling that that perhaps makes the seminar leader even more authoritarian because he's on his home ground.

6:   He sits behind his desk, doesn't he.

2:   We all try and crush in round the table or something.

5:   Sometimes the desk is facing the other way so they'll just swing round. But still with all his books there and everything like that . . .

4:   Yes, I think we were more kept down in that setting.

2:   We certainly weren't like on neutral territory, obviously. Also the rooms aren't designed for seminar rooms and you've got someone squashed in a corner and you can't sit around in a circle. It's much more cramped usually because their rooms aren't very big.

JR: But you can smoke presumably. Do you smoke in any case?

3:   In seminars? Oh yes.

4:   It depends. Sometimes a seminar leader asks you not to smoke. (All talk at once.) As a smoker I've no objection to being told that I can't smoke, providing it's a rule and not a whim.

1:   I certainly wouldn't light up in a lecturer's room if I knew that *he* didn't smoke.

Timetabling and timing

1:   In this particular year you get a lecture here and then a seminar in yet another block and there's a distance to go between them all, and usually you miss the beginnings and ends of things. You just regard it as a sort of task.

JR: Are they timetabled absolutely end on?

1:    Only those three.

3:    I think it's very bad to go in even a minute or two late because you just don't know what you've missed. I feel I'd better not speak for ten or fifteen minutes, even if I think I know what I'm talking about, in case the guy has started off by saying 'Well, we'll ignore this aspect of it' or they've started off with a discussion that makes my comment ridiculous.

5:    But don't they generally start late anyway?

JR: This end on thing interests me because people complain in schools about kids having to shift from one subject to another, and here it is again. Because it seems to me that if you generate ideas in lectures or seminars you need time to reflect on them — learning goes on after the seminar is over, when you have time to reflect.

1:    In the case of these three in a row, as I said, it's a task. It's sort of mechanical. I go through it and I don't think too much about it. I come out at the end and I think 'Phew! Quick, a coffee' and you don't think about anything that went on in the seminar afterwards.

5:    But what's the alternative? Is the alternative that you have an hour between each? Well, we'd all agree that that's as bad. I do object to having an hour between things. It makes you waste the day. There's not much you can do in an hour.

.   .   .

JR: What about ending the seminar? If you've got another one afterwards you rely on it's being ended, but do you see it as the seminar leader's responsibility to end the seminar? If it goes on over time, do you feel you can get up and go?

3:    Well, people tend to feel nervous about getting up while the guy is talking or while there's still discussion going but very often when it comes towards time people seem to shut up anyway.

Group size

JR: Just a quick comment on group size. What, for you, is the ideal size? (The responses are '9', '8', 'less than 10', '6'.)

4:    It's okay in a group like this having half a dozen because we'll all talk, but in a normal seminar group only two or three of us would be talking.

2:    It's the difference of the material we're discussing. Something we're discussing now we're not going to be assessed on. That's not really what I'm getting at, I don't think. It's all right when you're dealing with feelings or experiences but dealing with something in a seminar that's about something you've read, I find it difficult to talk on this critical, intellectual type basis.

4:    We're less nervous in a thing like this because we're only talking about it because we want to and we're only speaking about it if we know about it, whereas in a lot of seminars we're talking about things that you don't know very much about and you're supposed to have done some reading and you probably haven't so you're much more careful because you don't want to make a fool of yourself.

.   .   .

2:    You don't often get embarrassing silences in a small group.

4:    I think it's worse in a big group. In these seminars we quite often have embarrassing silences and there are about thirty of us there and that was quite embarrassing.

3:    If it's too big you're afraid to talk because you don't know so many of the people around you.

4:    You don't want to make a fool of yourself, in the large group.

3:    That's right, yes.

5:    You feel somebody might catch you out in thirty whereas they might not if there's half a dozen. (laughter)

2:    When I said it was more embarrassing in a small group, well it doesn't happen so often in a small group, but when it does, when people have all stopped at once, it's real difficult.

1:    But does it really matter that much because if you're a sort of group that usually talks quite a lot and you come to a full stop, then surely that should be a signal to the seminar leader that you've finished with that topic?

5:    But there's more than one kind of silence, isn't there? I think I was differentiating an embarrassed silence from that kind of silence which is a sort of conclusive silence. A conclusive silence is okay. That's not embarrassing.

6:    It's when a seminar leader says, 'Now what do you all think of this?' And you go . . . (she whistles) (laughter) It's when you know someone's *got* to say something.

JR: Is there anything else you feel you'd like to say about working in small groups that you haven't said? (silence)

3:    That's a typical reaction at the end of the seminar. (laughter)

5:    That is a valid point — that a direct question like that tends to produce a silence because people generally have to think and the trouble is that somebody often rushes in and says something.

JR: Or it may be my way of stopping the discussion! I wasn't thinking of it then, but I suddenly saw that it *is* a discussion stopper!

CHAPTER V   MONITORING SMALL GROUP WORK

THE ISSUES

It is not possible to respond, in the impersonal pages of a book, to all the vivid and peculiar dilemmas that seminar leaders may be burdened with. As Miles points out, seminar leaders have such a range of 'specific problems and gripes':

' "How do you handle the person who talks all the time?"

"What can be done about apathy?"

"I don't know what to do when there is a clash of personalities."

"What is the best way to start off a meeting?"

"How about the person who goes off on tangents constantly?"

"How do you avoid making mediocre decisions in groups?" '
(1959, p. 23)

The discussion that follows is based on the assumption that the most productive way to proceed is to help the seminar leader to be her own physician: to suggest ways in which she might sharpen her perception of what is going on in her seminar groups, and help her to increase her powers of diagnosis and become adventurous in considering what action she might take to improve the state of health of her seminars.

The monitoring of group work is not recommended as a persistent preoccupation. Analysis is at most an occasional regimen. Over-indulgence can lead to frantic dependence and to the kind of ridicule that Malcolm Bradbury offers in his novel of university life, *The History Man:*

'Classes at Watermouth are not simply occasions for the one-directional transmission of knowledge; no, they are events, moments of communal interaction . . . For Watermouth does not only educate its students; it teaches its teachers. Teams of educational specialists, psychologists, experts in group dynamics, haunt the place; they film seminars, and discuss them, and, unimpressed by anything as thin as a manifestation of pure intellectual distinction, demonstrate how Student C has got through the class without speaking, or Student F is expressing boredom by picking his nose, or Student H has never, during an hour-long class, had eye-contact with the teacher once.'
(1975, pp. 127-8)

Miles (1959, pp. 24-5) makes a more reasoned statement when he argues the need for moderation in self- or group-monitoring procedures: 'Otherwise our groups would everlastingly be caught in involuted analyses of who did what to whom, and group tasks would never get done. A good group member, then, operates habitually much of the time – he notes missing functions and supplies them almost automatically. Most of his energy, as it should, goes into thinking about the content of the discussion and contributing his ideas.'

1.   *Authority in relation to student participation*

(Sections 1 to 4 are largely a summary of points made earlier in the book.)

It seems, from first hand experience and the reported experience of others, that problems in participation are in large part traceable to the functioning of authority in group work. It may be the authority of knowledge, of the institution and its ways, or of the teacher herself. The immediate concern in this section is with the authority of the teacher. The basic assumptions are that authority is likely

– 	To induce a dependent relationship between students and staff.

– 	To foster strategies which minimise risk-taking and maximise personal security.

If this formulation is valid, then it is important that students and teachers find ways of breaking down the mutually reinforcing factors of dependence and security. Crudely put, the central problem is to ensure that the seminar leader's authority – vested in her age, her expertise, and her institutional position – does not baulk adventurous thinking and participatory learning.

The seminar leader may decide to weaken dependence by adopting a strictly interpreted chairman's role. In this role

– 	The seminar leader would be watchful for relevance.

– 	She would be mindful of standards (i.e. in calling for appropriate substantiation of opinion).

– 	She would help the group to consider relevant evidence.

– 	She would help the group to be reflective in discussion.

– 	She would weigh the needs of an individual in relation to the needs of the group.

– 	She would ensure that from time to time the focus of the discussion was clarified and, where appropriate, the range of views expressed was summarised.*

- She would ask questions rather than make statements, unless the statements were about procedure.

- She would be concerned that minority views have a hearing.

- She would be concerned to protect divergence (unless consensus were a legitimate outcome to the task).**

What follows are lists of behaviours or events that the seminar leader may need to be watchful of in the group situation.

a.   *Signs of student dependence on the seminar leader*

- The contributions of the students are directed to the seminar leader; there is little or no cross-group discussion. Eyes are fixed on the seminar leader.

- Students take notes, but only following a contribution made by the seminar leader. Little attention is paid to the remarks of other students.

- Student contributions constitute less than half the total talk of the group.

- Students try to force the seminar leader to work through the agenda in a series of mini-lectures.

- Students throw back the seminar leader's questions, seeking, through clarification, the 'right' or 'expected' answer.

b.   *Moves by the seminar leader that might inhibit participation by students*

- The seminar leader opens the session with an 'investigation' into work done. (In a competitive ethos, such an opening carries the threat of exposure. Anxiety may be intensified when the seminar leader is also the assessor. It is interesting to observe how difficult it is for students to talk about their work.)

---

*And yet summarising may, in some circumstances, reinforce a dependent relationship:

'A technique often used by leaders to give structure and direction is the periodic summary of points and arguments. The effects of this technique are uncertain. On the one hand, the leader is often in the best position to *extract* a pattern from remarks which may seem to the students to be random. 'Flag waving' when a pattern or point is being missed may well be essential. On the other hand, there is a danger that the leader will *impose* a pattern on recalcitrant material and lead attention back to himself. The balance is delicate.'

(Internal, unpublished discussion paper prepared by Alan Hobbs, 1972.)

**Committees have chairmen. A committee generally seeks a consensus or majority decision which will endorse action; in small group work, however, the aim is more often the protection of divergence in the interests of individual understanding.

- The seminar leader opens the session with an extended – and learned – contribution and there is no opportunity for a student to speak for some minutes. During the course of the seminar, lengthy, articulate monologues by the seminar leader are likely to make it difficult for students to move back into discussion (for one thing, students are often uncertain whether, in fact, the speaker has finished).

- The seminar leader interrupts students (and is generally not interrupted by students).

- The seminar leader fairly often rephrases student contributions ('You mean . . .'). Students rarely have the temerity to disagree. She might instead call for clarification by the student and encourage students to seek clarification of each other.

- The seminar leader asks questions to which she knows the answer (and which are therefore designed to elicit an anticipated answer) rather than questions to which she does not know the answer. Her questions are seldom born of genuine puzzlement.

- The seminar leader exerts power through language. She may be much more competent in talk than her students. She may, if she enters the debate, confound them with style. A phenomenon of early first-year undergraduate discussions are the *sotto voce* responses and halting delivery of the students. The seminar leader may need to temper her style until she is sure that students can cope with it. She may even have to develop a hesitancy tactic which would slow down the pace of discussion and enable slower thinkers to take part – it might also reduce the impression of her verbal invulnerability.

- The seminar leader 'pounces' ('What do you think, John?'). Pounces are likely to inhibit discussion in two ways: they signal that the initiative is with the seminar leader to cue in the students, and they can appear threatening (traditionally, the secondary school 'pounce' is an indirect way of rebuking an inattentive student). The direct invitation to contribute needs to be sensitively used. It should follow a signal that John *wants* to talk but has difficulty in finding space or nerve. And yet, if the very timid student does not contribute in the early part of the course, he will find it increasingly difficult to take part as time goes on. There may be a case for the seminar leader making opportunities, in an early meeting, for all students to talk, bringing each in on a known area of interest or expertise.

- The seminar leader communicates, through language or gesture, boredom or low expectations of the group's achievement.

2. *Questioning behaviour in relation to student participation*

A sound index of students' growing independence in the group is when they begin to question each other or to question the seminar leader. Questioning often seems to be the prerogative of the seminar leader. There are some moves, related to the authority of the teacher, that are likely to inhibit discussion:

—   The closed question, where there is one answer, and where it seems that the seminar leader knows the answer.

—   Questions which call for yes/no answers, and which are likely to throw initiative back to the seminar leader.

—   The open question, but where the seminar leader ignores some promising responses, and narrows pursuit to lines that appear to support her own interests or position.

—   The multiple question that blurs the lines of possible response.

—   The complex question which *may* be understood by the group, but which the seminar leader rephrases before the students have had time to think out a response.

—   The personal question: questions that probe the personal experience of students can seem intrusive. Students may clam up. If a student offers very personal data, it may be difficult for other students to find strategies for responding critically and intellectually to the evidence.

—   The direct question: a student will tend to evade a direct question from the seminar leader — and other students tend not to come in and offer responses. If the question has implications that are important for the enquiry, then it may need to be re-introduced at a later stage.

—   The phatic question: questions such as 'Is everyone happy with that?' may suggest that consensus, or understanding, *ought* to have been achieved. They may prevent the acknowledgement of puzzlement, or indicate that the leader wants to move on. If the seminar leader is genuinely concerned to ensure that everyone has understood, then it might be more fruitful for her to invite difficulties: 'I'm not sure that all the puzzles are cleared up yet; would anyone like to voice any uncertainties?'

3. *Pace and timing in relation to student participation*

The pace of discussion and the handling of silence can affect the pattern of student participation:

—   The seminar leader who is not sensitive to pace, and to the space between words, is likely to find that discussion becomes, if not competitive, then the monopoly of the quick and articulate — and the quick and articulate do not necessarily manage depth and wisdom. The seminar leader needs to be mindful of the need for thinking time. It may be prudent sometimes to shift briefly out of talk and into writing. Writing is a brake on headlong speed, and it can reduce the dominance of individual members and give non-dominant students a chance to summon and shape their ideas for presentation. The seminar leader may need to legitimise quiet moments.

—   Silence — the silence of non-response rather than the silence of a group reading or thinking — can be used by the group as a weapon to induce the seminar leader to take over and do the work. The seminar leader may need to learn to keep her nerve and not to break silences which do *not* seem to be the result of misunderstanding. (Silences that follow multiple questions or lengthy statements by the seminar leader may well indicate genuine uncertainty and the seminar leader may have to come in and help the group to re-focus.)

—   The seminar leader might, in order to increase the variety of pace and range of experience in the seminar, wish to encourage periods of silent reading. If she does so, she has to be sure to give the group time enough to read the text in question, and to legitimise the period of quiet so that students do not feel an obligation to ease the silence by making odd comments as they read or by trying to engage in debate with the seminar leader while others are still reading. Reading in a group is generally difficult to achieve — as is the transition from reading to discussion — unless it is clear to the group why they are reading the text in question: is it a directed reading where the task is to find evidence to illuminate a particular issue, or is it a more open reading where the range of response will be the stimulus to and subject of further discussion?

4.   *Support for the self-monitoring seminar leader*

Two checklists are given below. The theoretical assumption underlying them is that the authority of the seminar leader influences both the opportunities for participation and the manner of participation. The lists focus attention on specific behaviours of the seminar leader which tend to be coloured by her authority. They draw on points already made:

a.   *Points for the seminar leader to bear in mind when considering her interventions in discussion*

—   Are you consistent in chairmanship? Are all students treated with equal respect, and are all views heard with equal respect?

—   Are silences generally broken by you? Is your interruption a contribution
      to the task of the group or is it more a matter of easing out of an awkward
      silence?

—   Do you often interrupt students while they are speaking? What is your
      purpose? What are the effects of your interruption?

—   Do you often repeat a student's contribution? What are the effects?

—   Do you move the group, inadvertently, towards consensus? Compare the
      effect of the question 'Do we all agree?' with the effect of questions such
      as 'Does anyone disagree with that?', 'Can anyone see another possible view/
      interpretation?', 'What do other people think?'.

—   Do you habitually confirm student contributions? Do you say 'yes' or 'no'
      or 'that's right' or 'good'? What is the effect of this? Is there any evidence
      that students are looking to you for rewards rather than to the task?

—   To what extent do you ask questions where you know the answer? Compare
      the effects of asking such questions with the effects of questions to which
      you do not know the answer.

—   Do you correct errors of information on the part of the student? What is
      the effect of the tactic you use?

—   Are you reliable about time? Do you observe the ending of the session as
      strictly as the beginning — so that students can be sure how much time they
      have left?*

b.   *A focus on common interventions*

The statements/exclamations/questions below are quotations from a discussion
(on drugs) among secondary school students — but the general implications are
probably still valid for discussion work in higher education. (This is not to say
that we would endorse the marks allocated in all cases!)

The following teacher behaviours are roughly evaluated on a scale of plus five to
plus thirty for more freeing responses and minus five to minus thirty for more
inhibiting responses:

—   That's right — 25

---

*This list was derived from a self-training procedure for teachers who are handling controver-
sial issues, in discussion, in secondary schools. The items printed above are those that seemed
most relevant for small group work in higher education. (See Humanities Curriculum Project,
1970, pp. 27-9)

—   That's wrong — 25

—   Gasp! — 25

—   Good — 25

—   Look that up in the reference book — 15

—   Now that isn't what I told you last time — 25

—   I know you don't mean that — 25

—   The fact is that people die of heroin every day — 20

—   Where did you get that information? — 25

—   Can you prove that? — 25

—   What do you think? (To a pupil who has asked the teacher a question) + 25

—   I agree — 25

—   I disagree — 25

—   That's nonsense — 30

—   Yes? (To the group, after an extended silence) + 25

—   Does anyone else have anything to say? + 10

—   Now that makes sense — 25

—   Let him finish his thought + 15

—   Isn't anyone going to answer his question? — 10

—   Are you all going to ignore what he said? — 10

—   Now let's discuss that point for a few minutes — 25

—   Oh, is that so? — 20

—   (Silence without facial expression) + 30

—   (Repeating a student's comment without emotion or comment of your own but only after extended silence) + 25

– It's all right to say what you feel + 30

– It's all right to say what you think + 30

– How many agree with that? Raise your hands – 30

– How many disagree with that? Raise your hands – 30

– Everybody doesn't have to agree + 20

– That's why John gets A's on his paper – 25

– I don't know + 30

– I won't answer any questions during this discussion + 30
  (Epstein, 1972, pp. 33-4)

5. *Eliciting feedback from the group*

The security (or insecurity) that the seminar leader may feel about the *group's* progress and well-being (as opposed to her *personal* sense of security or insecurity in the group) may be illusory. It is enormously difficult, unless the seminar leader is very experienced, to 'read' the group. The seminar leader may form an impression of the feelings of individual students whose responses are readily demonstrated and she may use these students as a weather vane for the total group.

It is difficult for the seminar leader to be sure of her interpretations of the group's sense of achievement because her more broadly-based knowledge may be used to weave student contributions into a pattern that is more coherent and satisfying than students would perceive it to be. As one seminar leader said: 'I forget that the bits and pieces have come from different directions, that *I* have filled in the gaps, that *I* have finished the picture.' The challenge for the seminar leader is to test her impression that things have gone well against feedback from students in the group. The problem is, how does a seminar leader get reliable feedback?

The experience and ethos of a particular group must be taken into account when choosing strategies for eliciting feedback. Some seminar leaders may feel that they and the group would feel comfortable with written comments – which, when summarised, might form the basis of a discussion (if time allows) and, subsequently, might lead to some serious attempt by the seminar leader at modifying the management of the group. (Students, in interview, have commented on their scepticism about furnishing feedback, suggesting that the seminar leader either ignores the data once the event is accomplished or does not know what to do with the data.)

Some ideas for formulating questions might be helpful.

First, a straightforward set of questions developed by Miles — his 'reaction form' — for use at adult training courses. The problem it addresses is: 'What factors affect overt participation in groups?'

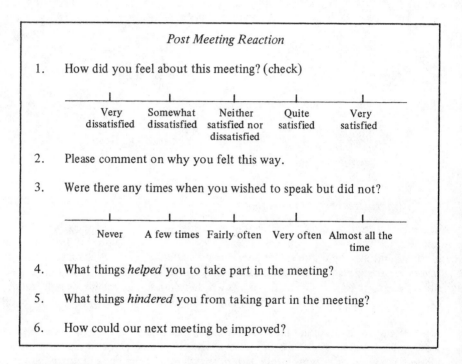

Post Meeting Reaction

1. How did you feel about this meeting? (check)

Very dissatisfied	Somewhat dissatisfied	Neither satisfied nor dissatisfied	Quite satisfied	Very satisfied

2. Please comment on why you felt this way.

3. Were there any times when you wished to speak but did not?

Never	A few times	Fairly often	Very often	Almost all the time

4. What things *helped* you to take part in the meeting?

5. What things *hindered* you from taking part in the meeting?

6. How could our next meeting be improved?

'Members need not sign their names. The reaction forms are summarized by a committee and reported back to the next meeting as the basis for diagnosis and planning (ex: "Most of the people who were dissatisfied also said they could not get into the discussion." "The most helpful thing was when we were in subgroups").' (Miles, 1959, p. 112)

A slightly more directed set of questions was used by the present writer with seminar leaders and students who had agreed to have their seminar recorded on video-tape. The comments were used as a basis for discussion in conjunction with a re-play of the video-tape. The response sheets were filled in on the spot and it was particularly important that the seminar leader also wrote down her comments and did not merely sit while students wrote, like a silent supervisor in a written examination. The response sheet starts with some rather crude categories which give respondents a chance to indicate their attitude without putting ideas into words. The focus on particular events was deliberate and, it was hoped, would provide a vivid basis for comparing students' reactions.

---

1. Would you rate this seminar

    Successful

    Fairly successful

    Unsuccessful

    (a) Compared with other seminars *within this particular course*
         would you say that this seminar was

    Excellent

    Above Average

    Average

    Below Average

    Poor

    (b) If you answered Excellent, Above Average, Below Average or
         Poor, can you give reasons for these estimations?

2. Were there, in your view, any extrinsic factors affecting the conduct
    and success of this seminar (e.g. – absence of key members of the
    group, were you feeling on form, did the environment help/hinder
    you etc.)?

3. Which were the most productive events or periods of discussion in
    this seminar? Which were the least productive? Please try to give
    some detail – and perhaps explain.

4. Were there any incidents in the seminar which in your view hindered
    or helped it?

5. What, in your view, would have improved this particular seminar?

A much less time-consuming response sheet is the one devised by Fawcett Hill.
It could be used regularly at the end of sessions so that the seminar leader has a
longer-term sense of progress. It is partly a way of charting individual progress.
It requires that respondents give their names:

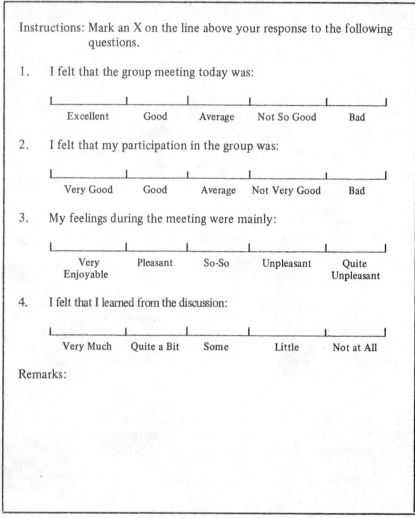

Instructions: Mark an X on the line above your response to the following
questions.

1.   I felt that the group meeting today was:

Excellent   Good   Average   Not So Good   Bad

2.   I felt that my participation in the group was:

Very Good   Good   Average   Not Very Good   Bad

3.   My feelings during the meeting were mainly:

Very   Pleasant   So-So   Unpleasant   Quite
Enjoyable   Unpleasant

4.   I felt that I learned from the discussion:

Very Much   Quite a Bit   Some   Little   Not at All

Remarks:

(Fawcett Hill, 1962, Appendix)

Ideally, response sheets should be designed to meet the particular needs of particular groups. An interesting exercise is to invite students, as a group task, to draw
up a list of relevant questions for a response sheet for *their* group. If the group has
designed its own questionnaire, then the task of completion may seem less onerous
or less of an imposition. Moreover, issues that are important to student members
of a particular group may not be covered by a standard pro-forma, nor anticipated
by the seminar leader if she is designing her own response sheet.

One has to ask whether individual written responses, whether named or anonymised, are really required, or whether, instead of being completed by individuals,
a response sheet might be used as the basis for a group's discussion of its work.
Alternatively, a useful starting point for discussion might be other people's criteria
for effective small group work. In these circumstances the moment of judgement
for the seminar leader — if the move is not made by a student — is when to make
the transition from a discussion of general principles to a discussion of the particular events of the group's own seminars. A simple and yet potentially useful set
of 'criteria for an effective seminar', which could be used as a point of departure,
is this:

1.	All members participate.
2.	Students argue among themselves.
3.	All students ask questions.
4.	All complete required preparation.
5.	All enjoy the meeting.
6.	Discussion keeps close to the point.
7.	Students gain some understanding.

(Powell, 1974, p. 167)

Finally, a checklist with a confessional tone — and a possibly cathartic effect —
but which is capable of leading lightly into the sober task of cooperative analysis
(it is *intended* for completion by individual students who mark column A if their
response is positive and column B if it is negative).

		Negative Roles
A	B	
—	—	Acted with aggressiveness and hositility.
—	—	Made self-confessions.
—	—	Acted with defensiveness.
—	—	Withdrew.
—	—	Sought sympathy.
—	—	Pleaded for a pet idea.
—	—	Horsed around.
—	—	Was dominating.
—	—	Did some status seeking'.

(Fawcett Hill, 1969, Appendix)

In Part II of this section are some transcripts of group feedback discussions where the stimuli of written questions or printed lists of criteria are not used. The transcripts show how difficult but essential it is for the seminar leader to establish a situation in which open and critical analysis can take place. Some assurance needs to be given that issues will be depersonalised for it is the seminar leader who is probably most at risk. (One seminar leader commented that he tried to give students an opportunity to be critical: 'Sometimes they could say most cutting things without realising how much their remarks could hurt.') Students have often acknowledged, in interview, that they are uncertain how critical they are expected to be (hearty invitations from the seminar leader to 'be as hard on me as you like' may not seem credible to the students unless the seminar leader's openness is consistent with her usual behaviour in seminars).

The seminar leader will also have to consider whether feedback sessions should be regularised – that is, whether they should be 'timetabled' and, if so, whether they should be held once a term, every third week for 20 minutes, every week for 10 minutes, or every session for 5 minutes. The more frequently feedback sessions are scheduled, the more important it is that there are visible attempts to modify aspects of the situation which have come in for criticism – otherwise students will see it as an empty ritual. Another drawback to a regular feedback commitment is the suspicion that time given to discussion of procedures is time taken from the coverage of the syllabus – and even in small group work the pressure of achieving coverage appears to be keenly felt.

Alternatively, the seminar leader – whose task it generally is to establish conventions, albeit provisionally – may choose to use feedback sessions spontaneously and in response to the immediate demands of the situation. In these circumstances she needs to be confident that the 'analysis' is not seen by the group as a 'telling-off' session, introduced when the seminar leader feels that the students are not meeting her expectations. Better if the opportunity for spontaneous analysis is one which the group can command, or at least one which the seminar leader will only use if she is convinced that members of the group share her sense that there is something blocking the work of the group which discussion might illuminate and alleviate.

The seminar leader would probably expect to, and be expected to, chair the feedback session, and she would possibly feel some ambiguity of role. One way out of this – if colleagues are interested and cooperative – is to make the feedback session very formal in structure and to bring in a chairman. The seminar leader is then able to contribute on the same basis as other members of the group. The colleague attends the seminar as an observer and takes the chair for the final twenty minutes. She first asks the students whether they have any questions that they want to ask of the seminar leader. The seminar leader is then asked whether she has any questions to put to the students. The chairman then feeds in a few fairly clear-cut observations of her own as the basis for a discussion in which seminar leader and students can all contribute. A transcript of a feedback session conducted roughly in this way is included in Part II.

Yet another approach to the problem of structuring a feedback discussion is to use video-tape. If recording facilities are available, the group might be invited to have one of its meetings recorded and to watch all or part of the play-back. It may be necessary to hold the play-back sessions outside the scheduled seminar sessions — a snack lunch provided by the seminar leader can provide an easy context for viewing and talking. In this situation the group tends to need some guidelines for viewing. If the playback is to follow the recording, students might be asked at the end of the recording to mention events or sequences which seemed interesting or problematic at the time, and which they would like to see on tape. Alternatively, a few issues might be identified by the group before the play-back starts (the problem of getting into the discussion, the length of the seminar leader's contributions, the relationship of seating to participation) which will give the group a watching brief during the play-back. In this way the students have both something to look for and something to contribute to the discussion after the viewing.

Video-tape is particularly useful in highlighting issues that the group might not otherwise have seen or which might be taken for granted. Here are two examples. The first is a collection of comments made by the seminar leader after watching a play-back of her seminar on the topic 'Art and Popular Imagery':

'(Viewing the tape) made a lot of difference to the way I teach. I tend to fill in where I ought to hand on sometimes. If someone is tentatively reaching for something, I see from the tape that I go 'bonk' quite often by giving all the information which they're reaching toward.

I'm conscious of myself as a new teacher in this seminar situation. And I think that shows there too. I see myself wonder: "Shall I let that go? Shall I go on with it?" A new teacher in the university situation — the anxiety forces you sometimes to say things when you need to be quiet, I suspect.

I don't usually define it (my role) to the students. I define it to myself as "the filler-in of information where it doesn't exist in what they have presented" — or "the infiller of information where they might not otherwise have been able to find out."

I don't think the students see me as an information desk. I don't know. Perhaps as an illumination of the object . . . One's dealing with an object and so one has to unpack the object in terms of the material that made it up, in terms of the concepts that made it up, and in terms of the background that made it up, so it's more a discussion of specific areas than it is dissension. The dissension arises more on issues like "Did x go to France in 1911 or was it early 1912 and how do you know?" . . . Dissension can come about by me making an extravagant statement that I hope someone will contradict.

There's a danger, if you don't (talk), that you end up with a completely apathetic seminar because they feel that you're not in any way interested. So you're caught in the dilemma of appearing apathetic whereas in fact you're trying to put the onus on them . . .

What I find works best is if I really do say nothing at all: someone says something; I don't answer immediately and someone else will find an answer!'

The second example is a collection of comments by students on the problems of communicating in discussion. The students have just watched a replay of their seminar on one of Kafka's novels:

'Some people come with their ideas worked out.'

'I have a feeling that quite a lot of people, myself included, had one thought they had in their heads right through the seminar and they're still thinking it through in spite of completely different things going on in reality. Especially if it's not cleared up properly, or if it's not really taken up.'

'I thought the sort of thoughts people were having – it didn't seem to me that people were really understanding what each other was saying.'

'I was trying to elaborate, but I see now that I didn't make myself as clear as I would have liked to.'

'(To a fellow student) It was only just today that I realised what you really were trying to get at. I don't think I understood you.'

'I was less concerned for getting one interpretation than for discussing various possibilities. A lot of possibilities were discovered. I think that's why it was successful.'

THE EVIDENCE

1.   *Members of seminar groups discuss their work*

The discussions took place during or after seminars which were recorded on video-tape. The discussions were transcribed by the author.

a.   *Seminar 1. Literary criticism: 'Hamlet'*

8 students (3 absent) following an honours course in literature.

Year 1, term 3.

The course was on literary theory and the group met once a week for a term. Half way through the term the present seminar leader took over from a colleague. The recorded seminar was the seventh.

The course was designed to introduce students to various concepts and methods in literary criticism and theory.

At the end of the recorded seminar the group discussed the seminar that had just taken place, and small group work in general.

Making constructive contributions in the seminar

1:    The fact that we can talk, the fact that it's not a mini-lecture, keeps our attention.

SL: Does it, does it in fact keep your attention? Sometimes seminars are very sleepy things, and move very, very slowly.

7:    Well, it's very easy just to sort of sit and say 'yes'. People just sit there and say 'yes' all the time and just agree.

6:    The fact that you might ask somebody a question keeps them on their toes anyway. It's the best way to keep somebody awake.

SL: This is a method very peculiar to me, that I tend to ask questions of specific people. How do people feel? Why did you think I was using this device? Did you resent it or did you think it was successful?

2:    I think you were doing it to draw certain people into the discussion, people on the fringe.

1:    Anybody can say what they think but if one person talks all the time
. . .

7:    It makes you think, that's all, if you're actually asked the question.

Otherwise you just sit there and accept what everybody says. If you're actually asked a question you have to think about it yourself.

.   .   .

6:      (referring to questions that are to the whole group and not directed at an individual) I got the feeling I was obliged to say something. Just in case nobody said anything. We all sat there sort of looking at each other hoping that somebody would say something.

SL: Is it just that you might say things to fill in?

6:      If one says something to just fill in they might turn out to be rather useless things which get the seminar into even worse difficulties.

Relevance and the seminar leader's responsibility

SL: Is there anything anyone got impatient about during the seminar, for instance?

4:      I was going to say I got slightly annoyed in that conversation about — "If your father had died would you be looking for the ghost?" I thought that wasn't very relevant.

SL: Should I have stopped it?

4:      I think it sort of petered out in the end anyway.

SL: Why didn't you come in and say 'This is irrelevant; this is boring, can't we go on to something else?'

3:      Well, it wasn't . . .

4:      I thought it was *your* task to do that as a leader. You know if you wanted the seminar to go that way, you'd let it go that way.

SL: So the way I want it to go is the way it's going to go whether you like it or not?

1:      It's up to us to tell you where we want it to go; isn't that the whole point of seminars?

SL: You're suggesting that this is a pretty dominant role, in that if I want to let them go on and you're getting annoyed about it, then there is nothing you can do. You just have to sit quietly until I get tired. This is suggesting that I'm a radically different sort of person in the seminar from anybody else.

3:    I think we all feel that. I mean, obviously we feel that. I think sometimes I get too frustrated. I say "This is irrelevant", and I shut up and a sort of awkward silence follows. One feels it is the leader who should put an end to it . . .

1:    It depends on us; it is us who have to say it – otherwise it's going to be like a lecture or a school where the teacher says "Do this and do that." Surely that's completely against the point of the seminar.

Structure in a seminar and the seminar leader's responsibility

8:    A certain amount of planning must be necessary so that people can have something to latch on to and to argue about.

SL: Does this mean that I plan and you don't? I am the seminar planner and you're the people who actually do the donkey work – make the bricks into a house? What sort of model would you use?

5:    The seminar leader must plan to a certain extent. Somebody has got to.

8:    Yes, you have got to have some framework for the seminar to work on.

2:    There are some seminars I go to where there is no plan at all and they always end twenty minutes before time and nobody . . .

7:    On the other hand you get some which are like a mini-lecture and you just sort of sit there and reams and reams of information comes out. It's probably all very useful but when it comes out like that it doesn't mean anything.

The logic of dicussion

SL: How coherent did people find the discussion was? Did we wander from one point to another or did the topics turn out to be sufficiently well defined – or too well defined, too regimented?

6:    I think this seemed to follow on. A lot of seminars, you say something and somebody else says something and you don't bother to listen to what they say. I find myself doing that in some seminars; I just sit around. If you think you've got anything to say, you say it, and then go back to sleep until you think you've got something else to say. Whereas this one, we sort of knew what we were talking about so the discussion was much more coherent.

Familiarity with the text

SL: What other questions would people like to ask about the way the seminar went? The way I conducted it, the way you reacted to me and to each other, and what actually got learned?

1:    Did you find it an easy seminar to take or did you find you were doing too much work, or what?

SL: I found it relatively easy. Partly because I knew it was a subject which related to work you began at 'A' level and it wasn't something totally new.

1:    I only yawned a couple of times and I usually spend the whole day yawning, so I think it must have been a good seminar.

3:    When it is a lot of new knowledge that you've got to assimilate that's when it becomes difficult. You want to sit and think rather than join in the discussion. You don't want to say anything until you've thought it over.

4:    Yes, that's a difficulty.

1:    Have a lot of people here done 'Hamlet' though?

3:    This is something, that before having a seminar you've got to have prepared it, because otherwise you are just not interested, you can't join in the discussion.

Learning about the seminar

SL: Well, two things are going on at once. One is learning a certain amount of information; I'm putting forward a certain spectrum of criticism but trying to get people to react to it in some way. But at the same time this business of training people to use the seminar, training people to come in and discuss — you think you are at a fairly early stage, therefore the seminar is still a very imperfect instrument as we are using it. People are starting to learn how to speak in seminars. Would people agree with that analysis?

3:    I think it's a matter of getting used to them really.

4:    I think getting used to *people* in the seminar as well.

SL: Were there times for any of you when the sort of inter-personal situation seemed to be getting in the way of learning? For instance sometimes someone may not understand something, someone may want to say, "Well, I didn't understand what the author meant; could you go over it again?" but may not say that, for fear of exposing themselves or fear of wasting other people's time.

1: If you want to learn you've got to be selfish.

2: To begin with, yes, until you get to know people.

1: When we know each other better, we will be used to seminars. Beginning of last term of course we were new.

b. *Seminar 2. Symmetry theory in chemistry*

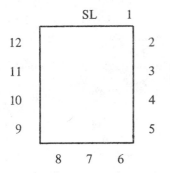

12 students (3 absent), all following an honours course in chemistry.

Year 1, term 3.

First of 6 sessions in course on Symmetry Theory. Four parallel groups met for two seminars a week for three weeks; no related lectures.

The seminars were recorded as part of an experiment in teaching symmetry theory entirely through small group work instead of through lectures and follow-up seminars. The seminar leader was interested in exploring a learning situation in which students worked largely in pairs.

Half-way through the course, the group discussed their small group meetings.

The difficulty of starting a 'let's talk about the seminar' session

SL: Well we're just over half-way through this completely different way of teaching a whole course. It's time to come to some kind of impression, or take stock, of how effective it is, how you like it, and in what ways you think it could be improved. So what I would like to do in this ten minutes is to get you to express your views as frankly, I hope, as you can. There's no point in pulling your punches. If you've got criticisms to make of me as a seminar leader, well, I don't mind what you say.

Just say it; I'm willing to learn. I just want you to say what you think and contrast it with what, what might have been put on, lectures, the usual kind of lectures and the usual kind of seminars. Right, it's over to you. I want your views please.

S*   You have to be shown how to do it in a seminar like we've got. I don't think you could apply it to all that many other courses.

SL: Yes, thanks.

S: Well, we haven't had any proper notes. We've only got these things handed out which we've got to read. Perhaps one should have notes.

S: It's not the sort of thing you can learn from notes. It's the sort of thing that you learn and remember (by doing it).

Learning in seminars and lectures

SL: What do you think of it as a teaching vehicle?

S: Well, it's not bad really. You can drop off to sleep half way through lectures. Seminars are so utterly boring it's unbelievable, whereas this gets your attention.

SL: If I were lecturing this, the point which we have now reached after four seminars I would have reached (I used to lecture this anyhow) after about an hour and a half. Do you feel that you've probably got it better as a result of spending four hours going through it in detail? Is the extra time worth it do you suspect?

S: Yes . . .

SL: Pardon?

S: We don't know yet. (laughter)

SL: What about seminars in general? I think you've stayed awake, and I think you've been working most of the time.

S: I think this pair system is good, all working in pairs.

SL: You like that, do you? Could you do that in an ordinary seminar? Could an ordinary seminar be so arranged to pair you?

---

*Note: The video-tape was accidentally wiped before the students could be identified.

S: It depends . . .

S: It would have to be rearranged. I mean, at present the seminar is just revising what is in the previous lecture of the week, whereas this is like a content which is thought out beforehand so you come in to it and go straight through and find that you're actually learning things in this method whereas in a normal seminar you don't learn anything at all, you're just revising problems.

SL: So you prefer a seminar which is structured from the point of view of content as far as I can see and from the point of view of contact with your fellows. So it isn't just me sitting here talking to you and trying to pull the occasional phrase out of you and you trying hard to stay awake. What about lectures? Now this is rather important because, you see, we can use this as a substitute for lectures but we're getting through the materials much more slowly. That's inevitable I'm sure. Hopefully we are getting through it better, but what about it from your side? Are the compensations really worth it?

S: Lectures seem too formal really and as this is informal you tend to get a lot more from it.

SL: What about you? You haven't said anything. How do you feel?

S: Well, provided you've got a reasonable amount of back up material to read and it's comprehensive, you have got an advantage with this informal seminar because in a lecture if you, you know, miss a certain point it's carried right through and you are without it.

S: Mm, oh, I agree. I think you really need the models in front of you. You couldn't do this in a lecture. You need the models there so you can visualise it. I find it quite difficult doing the homework without models. I spend quite a long time with it.

S: It's better than a lecture.

SL: Better than?

S: Yes, because the lecture leaves me behind years ago, whereas I think I'm just about keeping up.

c.   *Seminar 3. Literature: 'The Waste Land'*

8 students (3 absent)

Year 1, term 3

The recorded seminar is the fourth and last meeting on *The Waste Land*. The group met twice a week for seminars and there were some related lectures taken by the seminar leader.

At the end of the recorded seminar, a colleague, 'O', from another sector of the University was invited to chair a discussion of the seminar and of small group work in general.

Participation and responsibility

O: What do you feel that your responsibilities are? Do you have a concept of responsibility in yourselves? (12 seconds silence)

2:    Well I suppose we have a responsibility if we want to say something or think something, to say it and not to just sit there — you know — to the other members of the class. (9 seconds silence)

O: Anybody like to ask another question?

3:    I would just like to take that up. I think if you are talking to a class, to a class of your equals, a certain amount of ordinary tact has to come into play. I mean if you are talking to a Professor you can more or less be as scathing as you like because for one thing he is being paid to be criticised and for another thing he is your intellectual superior, so you feel you are entitled to exert yourself to the maximum. But when you are talking to people who are just the same as yourself, it is much more like being (inaudible) just sitting in a circle. I am not sure that that's an unmixed blessing. Often you tend to restrain yourself because of that.

2:    You don't shout at someone "That's absolute rubbish."

8:    I am sure it has been known to happen. (laughter)

O: But do you feel in a session like that you are more talking to one another than to the seminar leader? I mean are you saying the session is one in which you are conscious of talking to one another and therefore are more tactful than you would be if you were talking to him?

2:    Mm, I'm conscious of talking to — you know — the other members of the student group, but I am not at all conscious of being more tactful because I think I'd probably be far more reticent if I felt I was just talking to the tutor because I'd be afraid that whatever I said would be squashed flat.

3:    I'm not conscious of actually being more tactful, merely of being under an obligation to be more tactful. You see the difference.

Expectations of small group work

O: Does that contrast with your expectations of the seminar in any way? Do you find that the kind of seminar that you've just had in some way contrasts with your expectations?

2:    Expectations from other seminars or, or what?

O: Well, I don't know where you get your expectations from. I mean do you bring them up to the University with you, or do you get them from other seminars? Probably both I think.

2:    Yes, well, I got a sort of idea of what a seminar was going to be like before I came here — well, basically from talking to a few people who were here and going to the School's Open Day and listening to lecturers talk about them. But when I got here they, I mean it's, you know, partly my own fault, they didn't seem like what they were meant to be like, and this one — you know, corresponded most closely to my idea of what I thought it was going to be like, so far. I mean obviously it's our own fault if we don't speak, you see, if we don't contribute anything.

O: And you feel there is difficulty with making a contribution?

2:    Well, I suppose one's always shy.

O: Yes.

2:    And it's often very easy to not make one.

O: When you say it's often very easy to not make one, could you say more about what you mean by that?

2:    Well, if a tutor asks a question and nobody answers, very often they just let the thing develop into a sort of mini-lecture. Well I know he's not able to just sit there and say: "You haven't done the reading, tut, tut!". I mean it's embarrassing to them as well as for you.

Assessing the seminar

O: (to the seminar leader) Do you feel you'd like to ask them any questions about the seminar?

SL: I think there is one rather general question which I think is the obverse of the question that Keith asked me, and that is — of course I think I am here being fairly representative in saying that I have a tremendous anxiety about the amount of learning that has gone on and I would like to know, well, has anybody learned anything, or perhaps a better way of putting it, has anybody altered since nine o'clock? (18 seconds silence)

4:    It's a very difficult thing to kind of assess isn't it, personally? I think the thing about a seminar is that it forces you to just sometimes articulate what before has been just kind of thoughts, ramshackle thoughts in your mind.

SL: I think this is what continuous assessment should be. I mean this is going on to another tack, but the real assessment, what really matters, is the one that one makes oneself at the end of each session — did anything happen? Am I altered?

3:    I don't think you readily change your mind about anything immediately. It's very difficult to say at the time, maybe, you were wrong, or even to discover yourself that something you previously thought was partly wrong. But, if something lodges in your mind, you may remember it later. That's the value of discussions like this.

The role and contribution of the seminar leader

O: What do you yourselves feel are the problems of the teacher in a seminar like that? How would you interpret the seminar leader's problems? (6 seconds silence)

7:    I think it must be a tremendous problem in knowing where to draw the line between bringing the students to know things through themselves when you could sit and tell them everything you know and then say 'Well I've read so and so and so and so, and something else which the students won't have read because they haven't had the experience of reading for so long', and I think that would be a very difficult problem. I think in our seminar leader's case particularly, he's very much aware that the tutor should be part of the seminar rather than merely directing it and sort of looking at it.

O: Would anyone else like to comment on these problems? (10 seconds silence) Does anybody sense their — I'm sure this isn't true for every-body; I'm trying to think back to my own experience of coming up to University as a student. Does anybody find a kind of contrast of worlds at all? The feeling that one is negotiating from one world to another?

2:   When?

O: The world of the — the seminar leader in a sense, in the University, is a world which has to be negotiated across to the world that one brings with one, or is that not something that you feel? (Pause) It's not, I can see.

SL: Well, I — this is the first sentence of Elizabeth Richardson's book about groups, you know: 'Education is a transaction across an age boundary.' I think that's terrific.

O: Yes, I felt we . . .

SL: The contribution that one makes, particularly in a case like this, is simply being old.

O: Oh, would anybody like to comment on that. Is he right about that? (3 seconds silence)

2:   Possibly, I mean — (6 seconds silence)

3:   It seems a little doubtful, if I may say so. I mean presumably the contribution which consists in being old is, must be, something to do with leadership, but you are trying largely to efface yourself — not to be a leader in the sense of what is superior but to be an equal. I should have thought that that kind of technique would help to release, would make it easier to release your intellectual knowledge, the contribution you can make intellectually, to cancel out the difference of age, but you seem to be saying now that the difference of age is precisely what you *have* to contribute.

SL: I can't get any further at this stage . . .

O: Perhaps that's the paradox that lies at the centre of the situation — having to find the tutor is in some sense special and in some sense not special: how to negotiate between those two.

CHAPTER VI   LEADERLESS GROUPS

THE ISSUES

1. *Interpretations of 'leaderless' group work*

'Leaderless' here implies only that a staff member — the seminar leader — is not continuously present during the scheduled meetings of the group. Of course, in her absence a student seminar leader may emerge and even while she is present leadership functions my be shared by members of the group.

In practice there seem to be three distinguishable approaches to leaderless small group work. In the first, commonly referred to as the syndicate method (see Collier, 1966), a large group of, say, twenty to forty students, probably a year group in a particular subject area, is broken down into small working teams of four to six students. The teams, which are stable in membership, work on a prepared assignment. At intervals the whole group is brought together for a plenary session at which findings or experiences are shared, and then the cycle of activity re-starts. This approach will be discussed more fully later.

The second approach is much less formalised. A single seminar group of 'normal size', say twelve students, occasionally breaks into smaller units in order to accomplish a specific task. The seminar leader may or may not intervene or be present. The task might take up only part of a session or it might take up a whole session or even extend into other sessions. The sub-groups of students would probably share their findings or experiences by exchanging written notes and summaries; or they might make an oral presentation, explaining their solutions to a problem and justifying their findings and procedures; or (in a literature seminar) each sub-group might act a scene from a play in order to bring out possible differences in interpretation; or each sub-group might display and demonstrate a model that they have constructed. This form of leaderless work differs from the first in one major respect: here, the whole group is the main working unit and the small sub-groups are only casual teams, whereas in syndicate work it is the small group of four to six students which is the main working unit for the course.

The third approach is one where a seminar group of, say, about twelve students meets sometimes with its seminar leader present and at other times without its seminar leader present. These sessions might alternate — especially if the seminar leader is in fact using this approach to free herself so that she can spend half her time with a second seminar group which is timetabled to work in parallel. The problem here is for the seminar leader to work out a way of structuring the sessions which makes the most of the alternations. It is likely that the session where the seminar leader is present will take the form of a 'clinic' where the work which the group managed independently is discussed, and then the work for the next meeting is planned.

The first and the third approach outlined above are generally prompted, at least initially, by economic needs. Small group work on a 12:1 ratio is demanding of staff. In syndicate work, however, one or two members of staff are able to work with a large group of about 60 students, and in the third approach, only one member of staff is needed to supervise two separate seminar groups. Although the pedagogic advantages of these approaches may have been considered, there has probably been some post-hoc justification. Powell's research (1974) on leaderless small group work offers some evidence of the possible pedagogic advantages — and the disadvantages. It is probably worthwhile to report his work rather fully — with the proviso that, as he acknowledges, his sample of small groups was opportunistically gathered, and his procedures for recording contributions were largely experimental. His findings are therefore not proofs but possibilities, to be taken into account if departments are planning leaderless group work, and to be tested against their experience to see if the findings hold in other settings.

2.   *Participation in leaderless group work: a research study reported*

Powell analysed audio-recordings of seventeen meetings of each of thirteen seminar groups at the University of Papua and New Guinea. Tapes of the early meetings were not consistently usable because the system of recording was not, at first, entirely reliable. The meetings were analysed for the amount of talk contributed by each member of the group and for the cognitive content.

In no way did the groups consitute a representative sample: 'If students and tutor agreed to the tape recording and they were able to meet at times which did not clash with other recording sessions then they became part of the investigation.' (p. 164) The groups ranged in size from seven to eleven students and the sessions lasted between forty-five and fifty-five minutes. Groups working with a tutor met once a week and leaderless groups (set up for the sake of the study) met twice a week — in fact once with their tutor present and once without. No instructions were given about how the meetings were to be conducted although it was suggested that the leaderless groups could appoint a chairman if they wished. The leaderless groups were generally given a topic to discuss and some data or questions as a stimulus to discussion.

At the end of the period of study the students were asked to complete a questionnaire and a sociometric test, and both staff and students joined in a review of the experiment.

The method of quantifying individual contributions is fully described in an earlier article (Powell and Jackson, 1964). Participants were assigned code numbers and the code was noted, for whoever was speaking, at a fixed interval of one second.

(A category system was devised for determining the cognitive contributions to discussion. This aspect of the study is not our main concern here. What is of interest is that the investigator modified existing schedules in order to achieve one which he thought would be more relevant to university teaching — one which included cognitive activities thought to be common to all seminar work and which used categories that university staff were likely to consider educationally significant.) The general findings of the study are summarised in this way:

'Tutors spoke for rather more than half of the time and when the tutor was absent many students doubled their own contributions and participation was spread more evenly. There was a marked emphasis on providing information in almost all of the meetings but in the leaderless groups this tended to diminish and there was rather more stress on argument. It is suggested that the use of leaderless tutorials be more widely adopted.' (p. 163)

The mean contribution scores for the thirteen tutors was 58.0% and the range was 27.8% to 74.0%. It was noted that a minority of students who did not talk at all in the presence of the tutor made some contribution in tutorials where the tutor was absent. The talkativeness of tutors is explained by Powell in terms of professional norms 'which pressure him to keep talking since he sees his job as largely that of instruction'. University teachers 'conceive their instructional role primarily in terms of telling and explaining . . . most teachers are poor listeners.' Students expectations of the role of the teacher as teller and explainer serve to maintain the pattern of interaction.

In interview, students and tutors were asked to list the advantages and disadvantages, as they saw them, of the use of leaderless group work for at least part of their course. Tutors mentioned these advantages:

—   Students are encouraged to be independent and to rely less on the authority of the teacher.
—   Students gain confidence in speaking out.
—   Students have more opportunity for the practice of leadership skills.
—   Students are more likely to raise questions which genuinely concern them rather than questions which they think they ought to ask.
—   Students are less reluctant to reveal ignorance in a group where only their peers are present.
—   Students are more able to learn at a pace which suits them.
—   Students are more likely to prepare for the session if they have responsibility for managing it.
—   Leaderless group work increases the variety of teaching methods that students experience.

Students mentioned many of the above points, but added these:

- The atmosphere is more relaxed and students feel able to speak more openly.
- There is more time for students to talk and more people contribute.
- Students learn to help one another.
- Students learn more from their peers and so gain a deeper understanding.
- The discussion in the leaderless group is more stimulating.

Tutors saw these disadvantages:

- An ill-informed student could dominate the discussion.
- Without a tutor to guide the discussion the topic might not be thoroughly explored.
- Leaderless groups reduce the opportunity for staff-student contact and it is therefore more difficult for staff to get to know individual students and the areas in which individual students have learning difficulties.
- Some students are likely to be anxious if they do not feel that the session has a clear direction and if there is no one present whom they feel is able to correct their mistakes.
- A dynamic leader is important if the meeting is to be successful.

Students were more pre-occupied with 'the correction of errors' in their lists of disadvantages:

- They are uncertain whether what they say is correct.
- Much of what is said is probably irrelevant.
- One student sometimes dominates the meeting.
- The group makes more mistakes if the tutor is not there.
- If the preparation has not been done then the meeting tends to be a waste of time.
- Students sometimes fool around and the meetings are sometimes poorly attended.

The main generalisation emerging from the study is this: '. . . as tutors tend to talk for about half of any given tutorial period, the time available for student contributions is correspondingly reduced.' Powell adds, rather innocently: 'It would seem to follow that if we want to encourage students to discuss then we should keep out of the way!' But this does not necessarily follow. An alternative conclusion would be that the seminar leader has to learn to control the quantity of her contributions and to manage her authority in such a way that students are able and feel able to participate more fully in a discussion which takes place in the seminar leader's presence. Another limitation of Powell's discussion of his findings is the simplicity of the inferences. Powell maintains that students learn from their peers because students are closer to the problem than the tutor, who 'often experiences difficulty in grasping just what it is that is puzzling a student since that particular problem ceased to baffle him some time ago.' This is a rather shortsighted dismissal of a real and widespread difficulty in teaching. Powell goes on to suggest that a recognition of the gap between the 'mental structures (schemata) of the students and those of the tutor' might offer additional reason for accepting the claim that students are better able to learn from the 'explanations and interpretations offered by their peers' than those offered by their tutor. The root problem is a serious one. Observation in this country suggests that it is not only the differences in mental structures that separate staff and students but also the differences in *linguistic fluency and confidence,* and often *style.*

Indeed, Powell fails to comment that one major shortcoming of the leaderless group is the absence of a conceptual model — which the seminar leader often supplies — for helping students to acquire the professional register appropriate to their field of study.

3.   *Syndicate methods: characteristics, pitfalls and pay-offs*

a.   *The method outlined*

Collier has done most to pioneer and document the use of syndicate methods in this country. According to Collier (1966, 1969) and others (Chambers, 1973; Lawrence, 1972), the approach has mainly been tried out, in colleges, in foundation courses in the disciplines of education (for instance, the sociology of education). In his earliest relevant published work, Collier describes an experiment in the USA in which he worked with two classes of thirty and forty mature students. They met daily at sessions lasting one hour, twenty minutes; the total number of contact hours for the course was thirty-seven. In this time, the students worked through ten assignments. (In a later experiment at Bede College, Durham, the course consisted of twenty-six, eighty minute sessions and the students worked through six assignments.)

In a recorded review of several experimental courses at Bede College and elsewhere, Collier outlined the characteristics of the method and the characteristics of the learning that takes place:

'The purpose of this sytem is to build small group work in to the systematic academic courses of a university or college where classes are usually of the order of, say, twenty to forty students in size. The class is divided into sub-groups, or syndicates, of four to six students each. These generally work more effectively if they are self-selected. They are issued with assignments to be carried out by them working in the small groups. Each assignment consists of two to four questions. Detailed references are provided for the students to work on. The sources may be books or journals but they may equally be tape-slide packs, video-recordings or other kinds of material. Or they may be first hand observations in the field. These various readings are distributed among the members of the syndicate by the members themselves. This part of the work (the study of the evidence) is usually carried out by the student outside the class sessions. The syndicates (meet to) discuss the questions that have been set and to formulate their views. That is the heart of the whole system. The tutor usually but not invariably circulates among the syndicates, asking questions, probing into the students' understanding. Another feature is that the syndicates then report their views, whether in written or oral form. The findings of the syndicate are then collated in some sort of plenary session for the whole class, whether in the shape of a formal lecture by the tutor or in the shape of oral reports by the syndicates, supported perhaps by duplicated summaries. The syndicate discussion stage and the plenary consolidation stage together form a kind of rhythm of study, a rhythm of exploration and consolidation, of open-ended discussion and possibly didactic instruction, of independent activity on the part of the students, and, in some cases, authoritative exposition on the part of the tutor. The reporting back is followed or accompanied by general discussion in the whole class. Finally, at the end of the course or at some subsequent point, there is an examination of, or some type of test of, the students' knowledge . . .

'The characteristics of the learning that takes place in this setting are first that the structure and boundaries of material are only partially defined by the tutor in advance of the students' study. They are of course defined partly by the questions formulated by the tutor and partly by his selection of references. But they are also defined by other sources used by the students including, perhaps specially importantly, their first-hand experience. Of course, some further definition is introduced by the tutor himself in his handling of the consolidation stage.

'Second, the students have experience of active collaboration in the academic task of analysing, sorting and synthesising the material of their assignments. So there is a shift in emphasis from assimilation of material given from outside to the active construction of views and perspectives. And students consequently begin to develop a more independent attitude and judgement.

'The students contribute not only ideas drawn from academic sources but a variety of points of view which are derived from their own different personal backgrounds and experiences so that an individual's understanding of the material is amplified and enriched by the contribution of his colleagues, and ideas which are fresh to individual members are sparked off by the members jointly in the course of the debate.

'I have found a very high degree of involvement is often generated among students by this kind of work. There's a concentration of attention in the discussion, a willingness to spend long periods of time outside class sessions and a practice of making active use of several sources rather than simply mugging up the minimum that they're required to.

'And then, finally, one of the things that I have noticed many times in this sort of work is that a more relaxed and personal relationship begins to develop between the tutor and the students. In fact, it's really quite surprising how students begin to respond in quite a different way to the tutor as an academic instructor.'

b.   *An experiment reported*

In 1970, representatives of several interested colleges met to explore the feasibility of introducing syndicate methods, as a collaborative inter-college enterprise, in their sociology of education courses. An agreement was reached, planning and preparation began, and Collier and colleagues sought financial support for a study of the experiment which would look at the organisational implications, the attitudes of those involved, and the effects on student learning. (Chambers, 1973) A common framework of topics was devised for the course and common study packages of material were compiled. (The time-tabling arrangements and the allocation of rooms are not, however, mentioned in the report.)

The study confirms the impressionistic judgements about syndicate work which were quoted earlier in this section. It also warns against making easy generalisations and draws attention to the importance of institutional differences, such as the varying basis of composition of groups; the attitudes of the staff involved and whether they are volunteers or conscripts; the general culture of the institution; and the resources, including library stocks, available in the college.

Of the four instruments developed by the project coordinators to gather data about the use and effects of syndicate work, two yielded more useful data, and the report focuses on these: an open-ended questionnaire and an attitude scale. The function of the chosen instruments is to orient the study towards an analysis of consumer perception of the process rather than cognitive achievement. However, some points of general organisational interest did emerge from the study:

—   Efficient administration is a prerequisite of effective syndicate work:

—   Some of the most effective assignments are ones where the material to some extent parallels the procedural problems that the students encounter in their syndicate (for instance problems and evidence that relate to role or to the exercise of power and authority). In addition, case-study material has a rich potential for engaging students' interest.

—   The plenary consolidation sessions, where groups report back or are reported on by the tutor, can be unsuccessful if they are not sensitively handled and carefully organised.

—   Students who are unused to learning situations where they have to assume a high degree of responsibility may suffer anxiety in syndicate work, and this anxiety may be manifest in a readiness to become dependent on the tutor when he is in contact with the sub-groups.

Other points of interest related more to student feelings about syndicate work. (Adverse criticisms were most frequently expressed in groups taken by 'drafted' tutors as opposed to tutors who were spontaneously interested in becoming involved in syndicate work.)

— On the whole students think they work harder than in conventionally run courses. (Comments were also made about pressure from group members; irritation with students who do not pull their weight; the need for more time to follow through the assignments in greater detail; unevenness, from assignment to assignment, in the work load.)

— On the whole students find that they spend more time on work relating to syndicate tasks than they do on tasks in other courses. (Comments were also made about the enjoyment of time spent on self-selected activity; the fear of wasting time because of a lack of direction in the discussion; poor organisation of resources or insufficient resources to support the sub-group study.)

— On the whole students find syndicate work less effective in preparing them for the final examination except when the consolidation phase is effectively managed by the tutor. (Other comments referred to the ineffectiveness of notes made by individual students or by the sub-group of students as a record of the syndicate's work, compared with notes taken at a lecture or duplicated by a lecturer.)

— On the whole students think that syndicate methods are more effective than are conventional courses in building an interest in the subject and in providing a stimulus to thinking. (Comments were also made about gains in self-confidence; having time to think and to express thoughts; the benefits of an informal atmosphere; satisfaction at being helped by fellow students in the working groups; the opportunity for getting an insight into the way the tutor's mind works.)

The authors of the report sum up in this way:

'Perhaps the firmest impression is that when the syndicate work is well organised, directions are clear and materials and literature readily available, the majority of students find the experience satisfying and appreciate the opportunity to exchange ideas with their peers in ways that have advantages over conventional courses.

'There appears to be a slight trend for repeats of the exercise to produce more favourable responses from the new groups of students and this would suggest that the tutors' increasing familiarity with the objectives, the administration of the exercise and their own roles within it pays off in terms of consumer satisfaction.'

The report was concerned specifically with syndicate work in sociology of education courses. In Part II students who have been involved in syndicate work in other subject areas comment on their experiences.

THE EVIDENCE

1.   *Students comment on syndicate work*

In a tape-recorded review of several experiments with syndicate work, students who took part comment on the advantages and disadvantages of the approach. The comments are taken from the sound track of the video-tape which was made by Gerald Collier and his colleagues at Bede College, Durham, 1973-5. (The transcription, and the selection and arrangement of comments, was the responsibility of the author.)

a.   *On the composition of the syndicates*

'It is important that the colleagues (i.e. the fellow students in the sub-groups) are of *your* choosing. You are not told, "This is your syndicate group", you are told "Sort yourselves out so that you can get people to work with who are compatible." '.

'If you're working with colleagues there's an obligation on you to get your piece of the work done, therefore you come together as a team. You're not being told by the tutor, "You must read" or "You must do", but you're discussing in the syndicate with your colleagues and therefore there is an obligation on you to join in.'

'Everybody feels they've got something to contribute, I think. It's not all the same people who do the talking every week.'

b.   *Comparing syndicate work with more traditional approaches*

'It's a change from the actual lecture programme and we're willing to accept it as a change . . . you know the number of people who complain about Friday morning lectures and the number of people who don't turn up.'

'Well certainly you learn more by the syndicate than you do by a lecture method.'

'When I've attended a lecture there's nothing between my pen and the lecturer's notes. It just goes straight through.'

'One of the good things about this method is that it's not just one person seeking out information and then imparting it to the whole lecture group but you have four different people or five different people, depending on how many are in your syndicate group, who are going out and seeking information along their own track and then coming back to the group and then explaining this round the group and discussing from four or five different points of view. If we were to make an investigation into a particular topic we would probably just go along the one tack, whereas in the syndicate method we are effectively being taken along five different tacks which I think is a lot better for us.'

'You could find two or three syndicate groups going away and just discussing it for another hour over coffee which you don't find after a lecture — people just wander out and go and do whatever they were going to do next.'

'In syndicate work I don't think many of us disliked it. Even the lads who didn't really want to work actually did some work, which was quite surprising.'

'I think really we spent much more time on the syndicate if you did it at an average level than one would spend on an essay because it just seemed to be more interesting and we seemed to get more out of it. I would say we did more work.'

c. *On student participation*

'I don't think in a small group of that size you can afford to have passengers.'

'There is clear group pressure on the passenger to at least conform, to at least internalise some of the norms and read something even though it's only one page.'

'Well, if there's somebody who says "Well, there are only two points I'd like to make", would you call him a passenger? . . . It depends on each individual's concept of his contributions . . . You might not get an equal contribution.'

d. *On handling the resources*

'It was to easy to fall into the trap of churning out the ideas of the person whom you've been reading rather than developing, in the end, your own.'

'Well, personally, I didn't quote word for word from the book. What I expressed was the ideas of the author but I didn't quote word for word. What I did was précis and summarise but you can bring in your own ideas in doing that.'

'I found my reading was guided because I was reading to answer the question instead of reading and hoping that I could answer the question at the end of it. I was reading more intelligently. By the time I had finished I was reading both more intelligently and more quickly — and I was making better notes.'

'There's nothing to stop you reading more than the bit you've volunteered to read either.'

'Often there's only one copy to each syndicate of a given book.'

e. *On staff-student relationships*

'It's rather a funny thing that when the tutor or the principal came round to the groups, if they just sat back and listened, everybody felt uncomfortable yet as soon as they joined in, then there was a bit of feed back coming and everybody relaxed and there was quite a good relationship built up.'

'I think it's much closer because you're sort of together. He's not standing at the front asking questions or giving out answers – it's a much closer and more equal relationship.'

'Our tutor is an exciting character to be taught by, and he in fact bounced around from group to group while we were doing our work and we always found it great because he could fill in the spaces where we were probably having problems.'

'I think you can imagine with some lecturers it would be a disaster. There would be no informality.'

f. *On novelty, independence – and some related anxieties and uncertainties*

'It was important to actually have the freedom to criticise. We were told "We're not giving you any gospel. There are no right answers in any of these books. Use the material but don't slavishly follow it." This was expressed by the teachers.'

'The main difficulty is getting people to understand the ways of doing this. . . . The first session was really a shambles because people didn't know anything about it but they began to get the idea by the second and by the third it was quite effective.'

'I didn't know whether the group was picking out the right topics, the major topics, the major questions, and secondly I didn't know whether we were drawing the right conclusions. There was discussion time at the end for groups to report back but often that didn't happen – there wasn't enough time . . . and if you'd come up with some conclusions that are written down and you don't know whether they're on the right things coming up for the exams, you don't know whether you've drawn the right conclusions – it may be things that will lose you marks because you've drawn the wrong conclusions.'

'You are asked to write notes on your reading but you're never asked to write a sociology essay or assignment. There is a problem here, that when it comes to an exam you haven't actually been asked to present the facts in the way the examiner will require them.'

'But in a sense this is something special. We're coming on television to talk about . . . there's a sense of something special. When it becomes an actual – you know if it's ever adopted as a set course what will people's attitude be to it? What would happen if you did this every Friday morning for a year — what would we be like at the end of the year?'

2.   *Some examples of approaches where the group breaks up into small working units*

I came across several approaches developed by individual university and college teachers as a response to the specific context they were working in and the problems that it threw up for learning through discussion. The common problems were these: the difficulty of developing worthwhile discussion in a largish group (i.e. of between twelve and sixteen students); the difficulty of ensuring in a large group that all the students had completed some preparation which would form the starting point for discussion.

The first two summaries are of situations where the seminar group (one with sixteen and one with fourteen students) was subdivided. The third summary is of an approach where a whole class or year group of up to sixty students was involved. The approach was described by the tutor who developed it as 'a modest experiment' in syndicate work.

There must be many such approaches in operation. The three described here are not intended to be representative in any way. They are included to illustrate the potential of this style of working and the way in which it can be adapted to suit particular circumstances.

a.   *Seminar group of sixteen*

I observed an interesting approach used with second year students studying English as a main subject on a B.Ed. course. The sixteen students were subdivided at the start of term into four groups. A whole morning is available each week for seminar work.

When I was there, Virginia Woolf's 'To the Lighthouse' was the set text. At the end of the preceding seminar, each sub-group was asked to read the whole novel and then to re-read a selection of pages that covered an event of some significance in the novel. The reading was to be done individually. On the day of the seminar, one week later, the tutor met the four sub-groups and explained the procedure: Group A would now read and discuss the passage read by Group B, and vice versa. Groups C and D were to be similarly paired. Each group had to formulate, and write down, three or four questions to put to their paired group about the passage that had been studied in detail. The questions were to be interpretative rather than factual, and designed to explore the relationship of that passage to the main concerns of the novel. The students had about two hours to work on this task — and to discuss together their interpretation of their *own* passage. Then they met as a whole group, with the seminar leader, for about one and a half hours. One group questioned its partner group and was in turn questioned — but the discussion tended always to draw in members of the other two groups. The seminar leader came in only to make procedural comments or to suggest additional perspectives that the groups might later explore, and occasionally to supply pieces of relevant contextual information – for instance, where a theme was a preoccupation of writers contemporary with Virginia Woolf.

During the last ten minutes the students discussed the approach, which was new to them. The general feeling was that the session had been demanding and worthwhile. The structure had provided a focus for their reading and made them feel confident that they had something to talk about. They said that they were genuinely curious about the way that students in their parallel sub-group would respond to questions and they felt that the discussion was reflective and not competitive, and that everyone had participated.

It seemed that there had been just enough sense of group pressure and group responsibility in this approach to ensure that the preparation was completed, both by individual students in their own time and by sub-groups of students in the time-tabled time.

b.   *Seminar group of twelve to fourteen*

I observed a series of seminars – on symmetry theory in chemistry* – where the distinctive feature was that the seminar leader regularly sub-divided his group of twelve to fourteen students. The seminar leader was a professor, fairly new to the university, and he talked about his work in this way:

'I involved myself in seminars in the School, firstly because there was a lot of discussion about seminars – if they worked or not – and I felt I could not participate in this discussion unless I had some first-hand experience; and the second thing was that it is very easy for a Professor to be remote from the students and I would like to get to know as many as possible reasonably informally. I think there is much less formality about a seminar than lecturing.'

He had earlier been concerned to reduce the formality of the lecture:

'I can't say that I find any particular keenness on the part of the students to interrupt. We usually say to them, "Do stop me", but they are too frightened to very often. I always try to stay behind at the end of a lecture for a minute or two. It is more difficult here – before I came here lecture theatres were equipped, chemistry theatres were always equipped for doing experiments . . . you would always spend two or three minutes fussing around washing your hands under a tap so that if anyone wanted to grab you they could. It is much more difficult here because once you put the chalk down there is nothing to do except walk out.'

**See pp. 91-93

He found that the seminar rooms tended to work against his aim of encouraging a style of informal and easy participation:

'The University gives you a long thin room with a long blackboard down one side so there is no alternative but to have a long thin row of tables. But I would try to make it fairly informal by wandering around, sitting on the tables and offering the chalk to the odd student if problems came up. It is difficult when you have got parallel arrangements of that sort to introduce informality . . . I would see informality as one of the possible strengths. Teaching can become a dialogue . . . In a sense I was learning what needed to be talked about in a seminar when I was doing it. This may be an important thing − that the seminar leader does not go in with too rigid, preconceived ideas about how the seminar should go; he should be fairly flexible.'

In the series of seminars that I observed, he planned to encourage active participation by asking students to work in pairs. Each pair had 3-dimensional, geometric models to work from. The pairs worked on problems suggested by the seminar leader and then formed fours to compare results. The seminar leader sought the attention of the whole group when he decided that a summary or explanation would be helpful, or when a new task was to be introduced. On these occasions, work at the blackboard secured a group focus and students contributed, where they felt secure about their findings, to the completion of tables or to the interpretation of formulae. There were no periods of whole group discussion, but the discussion in the pairs and fours appeared to be thoughtful and sustained. While students worked in pairs, the seminar leader wandered round, intervening on his own initiative to ask a question or make a comment, or responding to direct requests for help.

A colleague, who took a parallel group and who was attempting to work through discussion in which the whole group was involved, commented on the pairing procedure:

'If you want a description of it I would call it seven tutorials of two being operated simultaneously . . . Yes I can see advantages in the approach. For one thing it goes more to guaranteeing that throughout the whole course of the fifty minutes each student is participating more often and more frequently in solving the particular problems he's been asked to solve, whereas of course in my approach, if somebody chooses to drop off to sleep they are quite able to do so.'

The seminar leader who had devised the procedure also commented:

'There certainly were areas where I felt it was going to be impossible to work in pairs − I just couldn't conceive of a problem that they could be talking about. I had to do a lot of thinking so that there were things for them to do in pairs . . . I think that the pairing situation does give you (i.e. the seminar leader) an opportunity to withdraw. You can always say "Well, that's an interesting question: why don't you discuss it with the people opposite and see if they can help you?" '

He was aware that one drawback of the approach was that it was time-consuming and he anticipated, before the series of seminars started, that the pattern of work might change:

'I suggest that as time goes on I shall become increasingly a leader; initially I want almost to stay out of it and be in the background as a prompter, urger and suggester, and hinter, occasionally drawing the group together, but really I would like it to be a time of self-discovery, guided self-discovery . . . I suspect that it may be necessary to speed up towards the end if we are to get anywhere near. I doubt whether we shall do all we set out to do, but I would like to make certain that we reach a point where the students are able to say at the end of it: 'Well what we learned was very useful, we can see some use for doing all that . . ." '

Later, when the course was over, he identified careful preparation as a crucially important feature of seminar work:

'I think they (seminars generally) fail to work because there is a lack of preparation on either side. Students don't expect to get very much out of it if the staff are not very clear what they're supposed to give. If nothing else, there is quite a lot of thought and preparation put into these seminars which perhaps is the main ingredient. I don't know. I happen to feel that student participation . . . is an important thing . . . So I think that the fact that I planned that they had to talk to each other meant that nobody could sit out.'

(For a full study of this series of seminars see Rudduck, *Teaching Symmetry Theory in Seminars: a Study of an Innovation*, 1976.)

c.   *A 'modest experiment' with syndicate work: a summary of an approach developed by Peter Scrimshaw*

The tutor was concerned with the provision of a course in philosophy for postgraduate students of education who often have little or no previous knowledge of philosophy. Three assumptions influenced the style of the work:

—   that many of the philosophical issues that would be dealt with in a short course are strongly evaluative and controversial, e.g. moral, social and political topics concerned with education;

—   that in dealing with these topics in particular, a teaching method must be employed that respects and safeguards a student's right to keep his or her views private;

—   that the teaching method used should try to ensure that when a student does present a view, it is considered seriously and sympathetically by both the group and the tutor.

The philosophy courses are of fifteen optional units; students are required to take eight. Each unit consists of five weekly sessions of 1½ hours. 'The tutor can reasonably assume the same amount of time to be available for students to do required reading.' For the unit, each student is given a set of worksheets (usually one per week), a set of duplicated extracts from relevant philosophical writings and a set of duplicated handouts written by the tutor (as a substitute for lectures).

At the start of the 1½ hour sessions, the tutor introduces the topic briefly and the worksheets are handed out. It is made clear that the worksheets belong to individual students and will not be seen by the tutor or by other students. If additional data is required as students work through the items or problems, they seek it in their handouts or they consult the tutor. The students complete the worksheets, usually without discussion with their peers. As they finish, they move out of the rough circle-formation in the middle of the room and form sub-groups of their own choosing around the edge of the room. The tutor suggests an ideal size for the sub-group which varies according to the anticipated controversiality of the topic – the principle being 'the hotter, the fewer' ! The sub-groups are given a very general issue to work on which usually relates to some of the latter items on the worksheet.

It is pointed out to the students in their sub-groups that 'discussion may be improved' if people try to formulate and present views they disagree with, as well as those they support. They are also advised to try to work towards the generalizations underlying the possible reactions to the specific problems presented in the worksheet. These sub-group discussions continue as long as the students wish them to.

If there is a general desire for a collective 'closing session' the whole group reforms. This session may consist of individuals raising particular points that interested them or of the tutor posing a question which arose in one sub-group for general discussion, or, on occasions, of the tutor thinking aloud about some problem which struck him during the session and where he was unable to think of a satisfactory solution.

In earlier versions of this approach, the 'closing session' was used by the tutor to summarize the key issues and to bring out basic objections to the various positions summarized. This was dropped, as its attractiveness seemed to derive more from its meeting the tutor's needs than the students'. Commentaries still figure in the course, but in the form of duplicated handouts. This makes it clear that what is being offered is the tutor's conception of what should be noticed about the issue, rather than what the various sub-groups actually discussed.

Handouts with ideas for further reading are given out after each session.

The responsibility of the tutor in preparing the worksheets is to see that the topics open up problems that are likely to be seen by the students as serious and practically relevant; to ensure that there are no references to philosophers whom students have not read; to ensure that there are no technical terms which the students are unfamiliar with. (The tutor made interesting comments on the final point: 'Observations of my own and other tutors' behaviour during discussions with either students or colleagues suggests that the extent to which we use such terms and make such references is only very loosely correlated with the real teaching requirements of the situation. On the other hand, the degree of reliance placed upon these things does seem to correlate rather well with the tutor's degree of insecurity and his anxiety to establish his role within the group concerned.')

During the sub-group discussion the tutor may go and have coffee, or remain in the room out of earshot of the groups, joining one or another only when requested to do so. (If he does join a group he asks questions rather than makes statements and stays no longer than is necessary.) He may, alternatively, announce that he will be joining each group in turn in order to note ideas for discussion in the closing session. (He may decide to write these ideas on the board so that they are available to other sub-groups to consider in their discussions if they wish.)

A colleague of the tutor interviewed five students about the approach, and a passage from the transcript of the discussion is reproduced. The students are referred to as A, B, C, D, E, and the interviewer as X.

A: Well if this sort of subject is going to lead to a discussion afterwards. then I think it's better to start with a worksheet because that forces you to crystallize to a certain extent your ideas about what you are going to discuss, because if you just read something, then it can go in one ear and out the other and you haven't really thought, whereas if you have to try and write down . . .

B: If you have a lecture, especially if it goes on too long, it gets boring and you have someone talking at you and your thoughts tend to wander again whereas if you have got a worksheet it's a sort of shared experience and you are involved.

C: I think you have to to prepare the worksheet terribly well though because you want everybody to be looking at the worksheet on more or less the same level if you are going to have a valid discussion afterwards. I found the worksheets very useful this session, but the beginning of the last session, when we hadn't used worksheets before, I didn't know what to write because I thought what I was saying was too trivial. But I had to get over that, do you know what I mean, I had to get over thinking I mustn't write down trivial things because that was in fact what was required – for me to write down whatever I felt at first, and then discuss it later . . .

X: Would anybody else like to comment on this question, about learning to use them, about what you found were the initial problems?

D: Horrible fear that perhaps somebody else was going to read it.

X: Is it important that it's yours and you can hang on to it?

D: The feeling was that you were given such a short time that you wrote down the first thing that came into your head which was usually utter rubbish when you looked back at it afterwards but it gave you a starting point.

A: The thing is that things you think are very trivial or obvious and hardly worth writing down, other people don't find trivial and obvious, or they have written down something which to them was equally trivial and obvious but it was in conflict with what you were thinking.

X: Did you find on the whole when you came to comparing comments you had put in, you were surprised by the differences of view which were expressed in them?

D: I got very involved in doing my own worksheet, and then the discussion starts and then sort of great different vistas and horizons came up around me, and I had just been focusing on my worksheet . . .

X: Would anybody else like to comment in general – what do *you* make of them? I'm sorry I don't know any names?

E: I think it's a quicker way of getting into the discussion. If you have a lecture followed by a discussion, then maybe the lecturer may go on for an hour and there's ten minutes discussion. This is ten minutes worksheet and an hour's discussion; (in other work) it's not likely that two thirds of the people have actually done the reading or even half, and even then they have probably not understood what it's about, or have forgotten.

(The full account of Peter Scrimshaw's 'modest experiment' with syndicate work appears in the report prepared by David Bridges and colleagues at Homerton College, Cambridge.)

CHAPTER VII   TRAINING STUDENTS FOR SMALL GROUP WORK

THE ISSUES

'The basic principle is to place all the resources available within the group at the disposal of all the individuals within it. The group must feel that everyone's needs count. This is not easy to achieve within the competitive assumptions of our education system. Nor is cooperative working typical of most spontaneous groups, at least in our society. Accordingly, tutors generally have to teach students to work in groups, to value different styles and types of participation and to resist the temptation to commandeer the group to serve one's own needs. The problems of developing satisfactory small group work depends as much on student training as on teaching training.'
(Stenhouse, 1971, pp. 13-19)

. . .

1.   *Locus of responsibility: the institution or the individual?*

Institutions are only recently beginning to pay attention, in a regular way, to the task of inducting students into the forms of enquiry and instruction which they will encounter in their courses. This is probably understandable if the proportion of time a student spends in seminars is very small. On the other hand, the institution may assume that its predominant forms of learning are ones that students will be familiar with from their secondary or further education. But it seems (Genn, 1972; Rée, 1975) that the sixth form experience is, by and large, unlikely to be one which anticipates the spirit of group work as it has been described in this book. Genn's profiles of the secondary school teacher and the university teacher are very broadly sketched:

'The school teacher characteristically engages in much telling, showing, exhorting, haranguing, checking-up, and rewarding or punishing. He is said to "over-teach", to teach students through the examination in spite of themselves (Olsen, in Schonell et al, 1962, p. 216) and is variously accused of spoon-feeding students, of cramming in facts and of emphasising memory and drill at the expense of understanding (Gascoigne, 1961, p. 145; Morris, 1963, p. 10; Rogers, 1960, p. 19). The most inclusive description of secondary school teacher behaviour is probably to call it "hovering concern" (Alpern, 1966, p. 594). University teachers emphasise the need for students to engage in self-generated cognitive activity (Alpern, 1966, p. 591) and try to employ appropriate strategies for causing students to organise themselves for unsupervised independent study (1972, p. 83).'

The generalisations (despite the references) lack real credibility, but one feels that there may be some truth behind the caricatures. If so, the sixth form ethos is not in harmony with the aims of small group work (as described earlier), and Rée confirms this impression:

' "What is wrong with our Universities", wrote Bernard Shaw, "is that the students are school children . . ." For a sixth former the final two years of school are increasingly dominated by mechanical learning in order to get the highest possible grades at 'A' level. Exam questions are "spotted", model answers are practised, corrected, fair copied, and even in some schools learned by heart. This is not education, it is slot machine teaching. And unless these practices, and the attitudes behind them, are thoroughly discredited in the eyes of students before their university course begins, both may be carried over, intact, and the course which was designed to cultivate . . . will end by stunting growth. For it will be regarded as being what its name implies – a race, an obstacle race, slightly more demanding than 'A' level.'

An alternative to institutionally-planned training would be for individual teachers to organise an induction but there is little evidence of individual seminar leaders making a conscious effort to help students to learn to work in groups. Again, this is not surprising if, as often happens, a group works together for a comparatively short time; a seminar leader would be clearly reluctant to give time to training students in the methodology of learning if she felt any pressure towards coverage of syllabus. ('. . . one of the problems that we have is that there is too much information to disseminate in eight lectures so that the seminar has necessarily to be part of an information session' – said by a lecturer in Fine Arts.)

And if small group work were in fact to constitute, as it does in a minority of institutions, a major part of the student's course, the training issue can be even more complex. The student is likely to be exposed to a number of seminar leaders and the seminar leaders' conceptions of small group work are likely to vary. Is it feasible that institutions might attempt some form of induction which would at least give students some insight into the common ground which might be expected to underlie the different approaches to small group work?

Of course, it might be argued that secondary education, with its compartmentalisation of knowledge and its oddly juxtaposed periods of study, ensures that pupils adjust to a cavalcade of teaching styles. Although fewer teachers are likely to be encountered in the course of a university term than in a school term, nevertheless, the conceptions of role may be very different, even within the one department. Witness, for example, the comments of two colleagues, senior members of a university department, who teach literature:

'I tried to establish the seminar as a membership (not a homogenous audience, nor a heterogeneity of 'students'). I kept my authority on the subject, such as it is, outside – in books and in the lecture room on quite separate occasions. I kept quiet in class. Stillness was intended to make room for the members to fill. It also presented the seminar-leader as a neutral non-member for the anti-work forces in the group to focus on — anxiety about seeming zealous, or stupid or eccentric; irritation, desire to flee and so on. My idea was that by staying in a very distinct role, I would enable the group to emerge and exist. The role I selected was recessive, non-competitive; but perhaps its being distinct, and my staying in it, mattered more than its characteristics. When we succeeded, it was when I stayed in role. When we failed (as we very often did) it was through my ceasing to minister to the group. I would lose faith in their ability to work, or in mine to be a target, and I would start 'being myself' — impatient, didactic, urgently or engagingly 'teaching' and trying to be brilliant.'

.   .   .

'It is a seminar where students learn what drama is about through dramatic activity. The seminar evolves. It is, to use the current jargon, unstructured . . . Students often need things from the seminar leader. I am always concerned to make clear my views and I will frequently dramatise them so that students can grasp and use my over-bearingness as a means of coming back at me. This prevents the respectful passiveness which destroys the students' ability to be critical of the views expressed by their tutor in class . . . If students are to move beyond the level found naturally by the group then my ideas are necessary. To go further means to explore my ideas.'

To sum up: the organisational questions in training students for small group work are more easily listed than they are responded to:

—   where is the locus of responsibility? Does it rest with individual teachers or with institutions?

—   is training best achieved in a group which has been formed as a working group or is it best achieved through a specific programme involving, say, the whole first year intake — either within or across departments?

—   what is the optimum time for training — at the beginning of the freshman year or some months later when students have experience as a reference and growth point?

—   is training likely to be more effective if it is conceived as an extended series of meetings or as an intensive short course? And what pressures would need to build up before institutions would endorse the giving of so much time to formal training?

There may also be attitudinal problems. The seminar leader who sees small group work as essentially a spontaneous and creative event may feel antagonistic towards the idea of training, seeing it as an attempt to reduce what is exciting and unpredictable to a set of restrictive laws. And the diffident seminar leader may feel uneasy for different reasons, feeling (as was once said) that training might make students better informed and more perceptive about procedures than their teachers — who would then suspect that they might have some difficulty in maintaining control.

2.   *Approaches to training*

In Part II is the programme for an experimental induction course for students which was organised on a departmental basis. The scheme involved several members of faculty and all first year students. The forty students met in four groups for one hour a week during eight weeks of their first term. Each group was chaired by a teacher from the same sector who was attending, simultaneously, weekly workshop sessions on small group teaching and learning.

This course was conceived as a *general* introduction to small group work. Teachers may, however, need a repertoire of strategies for training the group in *particular* aspects of cooperative learning. For instance, we have observed in a number of groups a cluster of difficulties in the area of pace, timing and sequence that might fairly easily be explored and resolved. The difficulties may spring from a tradition of valuing liveliness in discussion above reflectiveness. Liveliness is characterised by speed and a bustling continuity of contributions. In fact, contributions seem often to have no clear relationship to each other; the contributors are probably competing for space, and remarks may be divorced in time from their cues. The quality of discussion might improve if the group were prepared to learn to use silence, to learn to listen, and to learn to respond as well as to take initiatives. One strategy for combating the speed and superficiality that are, together, likely to be destructive of cooperative participatory learning is called, rather alarmingly, 'the four-stage rocket'! One of its shortcomings is that it makes assumptions about the importance both of logical sequence in discussion* and of everyone contributing to discussion:

'Pre-test

Break up into groups of not more than eight.

Select an observer.

Discuss an assigned topic for five minutes. (The observer will record his evaluation of the discussion.)

---

*One seminar leader sees the seminar as a pool in which members of the group 'throw' contributions. The sequence of contributions is not judged by its logical development. Instead, individuals make private links as the seminar proceeds and what matters is the richness of the total resource which the pool provides.

Stage 1

Select a time keeper.

Continue the discussion for five minutes but limiting each person's contribution to fifteen seconds.

Stage 2

Continue the discussion for five minutes, again limiting each person's contribution to fifteen seconds.

However, before a person speaks, he must wait three seconds after the previous person has finished speaking.

Stage 3

Continue the discussion for five minutes, again limiting each person's contribution to fifteen seconds and waiting the three-second interval.

In addition, no person may say what he wants to until he has accurately reflected the contribution of the person immediately preceding him.

Stage 4

Continue the discussion for five minutes. Limit each person's contribution to fifteen seconds and wait three seconds. No one may speak until he has accurately reflected and no one may speak a second time until everyone in the group has spoken.

Post-test

Continue the discussion for five minutes, with no limitations on speaking. Have the same observer as in the Pre-test record his evaluation of the discussion.' (Epstein, 1972, pp. 48-9)

Yet another approach, this time at a much more general level, is through the introductory handout. The British Columbia Teachers' Federation prepared a statement for groups on the *modus operandi* of the seminar. It may be that a handout incorporating such basic points could give a minimal support to students who are new to small group work:

'1.   Maintain an attitude of searching for a solution. You are trying to find the best answer; not trying to convince other people. Try not to let your previously held ideas interfere with your freedom of thinking. Be on guard against the effect of your own prejudices. You will find this difficult but highly rewarding.

2.   Speak whenever you feel moved to do so (and have the right of way, of course) even though your idea may seem incomplete. If the answers all were known, there would be no point in exploring.

3.   Cultivate the art of careful listening. You can practise this by trying to formulate in your own mind the gist of what a previous speaker has been saying before adding your own contribution.

4.   Try to stay with the group. Discussion which strays too far afield may kill the topic at hand. Avoid introducing new issues until the decks are clean of the business under discussion.

5.   Talk briefly. Saying too much may cause people's minds to wander so that they miss the value of what you wish to express.

6.   Avoid long stories, anecdotes, or case studies, which only illustrate a point. It is ideas, beliefs, implications, and understandings which are the meat of a discussion. Listening to one person after another tell long tales of "what happened to me" can quickly destroy a good discussion.

7.   Be as sympathetic and understanding of other people's views as you can. If you disagree, say so, but avoid the appearance of being belligerent or threatening other people.'
(1970, p. 4)

'Ground rules' for discussion might also be useful to students but such conventions probably need to be drawn up by seminar leaders bearing in mind the particular style and task of their meetings. The ground rules may need to be reviewed and perhaps re-negotiated with the group after they have been tried out. Here, as an example, are the ground rules drawn up for a discussion of literature:

'Rule 1 :   The group may discuss only the book assigned for the meeting or books discussed at a previous meeting.

Rule 2 :   No participant may take part in the discussion who has not read the book.

Rule 3 :   Participants may not introduce outside authorities to lend weight to their opinions.

Rule 4 :   (The leader) may only ask questions. (She) may never introduce her own opinions or make comments . . .'
(The Great Books Foundation, 1971, p. 144)

It is interesting to speculate how generally acceptable and generally controversial such a set of ground rules might be.

THE EVIDENCE

1. *Students comment on the difficulties of adjusting to discussion work*

The passage is from an edited transcript of a discussion I had, informally, with six final year students.

3:    We have these seminar-cum-lecture things. I'm not quite sure how you classify those. It's led by a lecturer who may sort of stand and talk for half-an-hour. He also tried to get the group into discussion. It's less formal than a lecture in a lecture theatre but not quite as informal as an ordinary seminar.

.   .   .

JR: How do you know when it's shifted from a lecture into something where you are expected to discuss?

4:    You just have to respond very quickly.

3:    It all gets quiet! (laughter)

5:    ... I had two or three a week last term with ten or twelve people in the class where they were seminars-cum-lectures.

JR: Is that learning through discussion?

5:    Not really.

JR: If it's not learning through discussion, do you mean that you're doing things or that the lecturer is talking?

5:    Probably the lecturer is talking.

JR: So when you came into seminars and discussion work did you just kind of take to that naturally, like a duck to water, or did you have growing pains? I'm really concerned with how you help students to adjust to small group work if they haven't been used to it at school.

2:    I think with scientists you tend to do experiments with other people so that on that sort of level you cope, but actually vocalising in a seminar is quite a leap, I think.

6:    One of my courses was in a School where they're used to having seminars right from their first year and I really did feel that I'd been plunged into the deep end and I had no idea how to write a seminar paper or what. I wasn't given any guidance. I felt it was just the idea that seemed a bit daunting.

5:    I think this is one great advantage of being a mature student. I wasn't conscious of any difference at all. A seminar was a seminar and that was fine and it took me quite some time to appreciate that some people did feel uncomfortable with it . . .

3:    I think it's the first time you really get a chance to challenge established views. You read a paper and you're asked to pick it to pieces. I find it a little strange telling a lecturer that I don't agree with him whereas before you'd always listened to him like the word of God. I think that took a few weeks.

2.   *An experimental induction course for first year students*

a.   *The programme*

General Preamble

In this department we have assumed that students straight from school are able, without more ado, to adapt rapidly to academic study and to our seminar system. This assumption is questionable and we are beginning to see that we must help students to adjust. Below is the draft outline of an experimental training programme which will be tried out in the Winter term. Four groups will take part. Sessions one, two and three will not last longer than an hour. The remaining sessions will probably last slightly longer than an hour. Use will be made of video-tapes of Honours seminars.

This programme is *not* part of our orthodox Preliminary Programme. It does not count for course credit and no work will be required of participants outside the eight sessions.

Aims

(a)   To create an awareness of the strengths and weaknesses of the seminar as a teaching/learning situation.

(b)   To create an awareness of what is required if a seminar is to work properly.

(c)   To create an awareness of the variety of seminar situations.

(d)   To create an awareness of the difference between a university seminar and a school class.

SESSION ONE: INTRODUCTORY (Week 1)

Students emphasize that the barriers which grow up between faculty and themselves are great hindrances to learning and to free exchange of views. It is vital that we identify the nature and origins of such barriers and do our best to remove them. As it is difficult to do this in normal seminars, this session will enable the members of the group to get to know each other over a bottle of sherry. What are people's names? Where do they come from? Where were they at school? Who has spent time abroad? What is the seminar leader's history? How long has he been at this university? Is he married? Has he got children? What are his interests outside the university? What is the nature of his job? etc. etc.

SESSION TWO: THE LIBRARY (Week 2)

During this session, students will be shown around the library.

SESSION THREE: THE STUDY OF LITERATURE AT UNIVERSITY (Week 3)

Why study literature at all? Why study literature at university? How will the study of literature at university differ from the study of literature at school? What do we mean by motivation towards a subject? What is 'relevant' about the study of literature? Is there such a thing as long-term relevance? What do people in the group find relevant in the study of literature? Why study literature in conjunction with a minor subject? What minor subjects form the most useful complements to literature? What are we looking for in essays? How should essays be presented? What problems may be encountered in writing class papers and essays? What can be done about these? What is the point of using secondary literature? Why take notes when reading texts?

SESSION FOUR: TYPES OF SEMINAR AND AGENDA SETTINGS (Week 4)

There are many types of seminar. Some begin with a mini-lecture; some with a student paper; some are preceded by work in small project groups; some follow lectures. Discuss the variations. What are the advantages and disadvantages of the various types? Is there a right way of conducting and structuring a seminar? When is a seminar not a seminar? By whose authority is the agenda of any given seminar established? What happens when there is no agenda — a conflict of agendas? — an imposed agenda? How is it possible for a group to ensure that the seminar leader takes notice of the agenda which it wants to pursue?

*Video-tape will be used

SESSION FIVE: RESPONSIBILITY FOR THE SEMINAR (Week 5)

Responsibility for making a seminar work lies with the group as a whole — not solely with the seminar leader. The seminar is best suited to the discussion of problems – not to the acquisition of facts. What must a group do before a session to make that session go? What must the leader do during the session to help the discussion go? What factors at this university will inhibit the preliminary work (noise in residences; unavailability of books in the library)? What can be done to remedy such situations?

*Video-tape will be used

SESSIONS SIX AND SEVEN: PROBLEM SITUATIONS IN SEMINARS
(Weeks 6 and 7)

Some typical problems:

(a)   How can a person disagree and conflict with another member of the seminar without becoming personal or 'getting at' him? Is there an art of polite disagreement? In what does it consist? What should a leader do in conflict situations?

(b)   How can a group deal with a seminar leader who will not stop talking – or who will not listen – or who squashes people – or who talks above students' heads?

(c)   How can a group deal with a situation where a seminar leader and a student engage in a dialogue without reference to the rest of the group?

(d)   How can a group deal with a situation where all talk ceases? Is silence necessarily a bad thing?

(e)   How can a group help an excessively shy student and deal with an aggressive one?

(f)   What are the problems associated with reading out class papers? How can discussion develop from a seminar paper? What can be done if the class paper is unsatisfactory?

(g)   To what extent is a seminar affected by the setting and seating arrangements?

This list is by no means exhaustive.

In all cases, there will be a need for background material. Group leaders might consider inventing imaginary situations for discussion and setting these out on paper.

*Video-tape will be used

SESSION EIGHT: CLASSROOM TO SEMINAR ROOM – SCHOOL TO
UNIVERSITY (Week 9)

Superficially similar, the school class and the university seminar are fundamentally
different. What are the differences between a class and a seminar; a classroom and
a seminar room; a teacher and a seminar leader; a sixth-former and a student?
What are the strengths and limitations of the seminar as a teaching/learning situation? On what kind of knowledge does the seminar system place a premium?
What cognitive skills does it aim to develop? Does the seminar system aim at bringing people up to our standards or at enabling them to develop their own? Do
schools and universities value the same intellectual aptitudes? In an unstructured
system like ours, what kind of continuity should be looked for?

*Video-tape will be used

N.B.   The above programme need not be strictly adhered to. Participants should
feel free to go off at tangents and follow up their own interests.

b.   *The report* (A much shorter version is printed here than was actually
circulated to faculty. Comments have been selected to show the range – not the
frequency – of responses.)

    i.   At the end of the term, a short questionnaire was distributed to the
        27 freshmen who had taken part in the project. This asked the follow-
        ing four questions:

        I   How useful is a Prelims. training project? If it is useful, in what
            ways is it useful?

        II   If we decide to repeat the project next year, how should it
           differ from our practice this year?

        III   How useful was it to look at video-tapes of seminars in different
           institutions and different subject-areas?

        IV   Any other comments?

    ii.   10 replies were received. This low figure was not surprising since all
        four groups experienced a marked drop in numbers by about the
        fourth week of the project.

    iii.   Responses to Question I:

---

*Note: The video-tapes are from a set of edited tapes produced by the Small Group Teaching
Project (see references).

'It is very useful for showing the pros and cons of the seminar system and especially how the flaws could be avoided.'

'On arrival seminars were reported to be some kind of idealistic academic playground which they are emphatically not. Here, we had the chance to talk about them, and decide for ourselves what they should be about.'

'It is useful, because although we have a vague idea of what is expected of us in seminars before we come to university, we only really learn how they work by taking part in them. The project has given us an insight into the possible problems and our own role.'

'I thought it useful as a way of breaking down barriers between staff and students. It also helped me in seminars because I felt the seminar leaders were aware of the problems that faced us.'

'There must be some way of making the step between school and university easier. This was good in that we could meet a member of faculty at an informal level and see how different the liaison is between faculty and students, compared with the liaison between schoolmaster and pupil.'

iv.   Responses to Question II:

'If possible, it should be fitted into the daytime schedule. My group took place between 5.30 and 7.00 pm. on a Wednesday and mainly for that reason was not as well attended as it might be.'

'If possible, everyone should be involved. On the other hand, not everyone would want to be involved so it should probably not be made compulsory. How about some beer next year?'

'Perhaps we would have got more out of it if we had had four sessions in the first term and then some in the second term. As it was, we were discussing a lot of problems that *might* come up, not problems that *had* come up.'

'We would like to see a block of meetings early in term I, then a gap, then meetings towards the end of term II, to allow students to gain more experience of the problems. Also — less on "the seminar" — more on lectures, note-taking, the structure of the course.'

v.   Responses to Question III:

'Useful in that it made the one *problematic* fault of seminars, over-long silences, evident to the students. It provided a mirror-image.'

'Watching seminars in a different subject area caused difficulties because it was not easy to follow the 'intellectual' course of the seminar. We never really knew whether they were talking rubbish or not.'

'The tapes I got the most out of were those in subject-areas familiar to me — though the teacher-training one on a particular problem did show us how much easier it is to have a seminar on a concrete problem.'

'They did serve to highlight problems common to any seminar, but I feel that the tapes should have been centred more on the type the group has paticipated in — e.g. the dance group tape was a bit remote.'

vi.   Responses to Question IV:

'I think that the project helped me to be more aware of the aims and problems of seminar groups, both from the leader's and the student's point of view. It has made me more determined to make seminars I attend more successful.'

'We had a very useful session when we asked all kinds of questions about the course generally. I think the project was useful as it raised questions in my mind about the purpose of Higher Education and the kind of cooperation that is needed if we are to get anything out of seminars. I don't know if it's had much effect on my behaviour, but at least it has raised some important questions.'

'Another problem needing discussion is that of self-discipline. How does one allot time to study with so many competing attractions and discussions?'

c.   *Tentative conclusions*

The approach seems useful, but many things need improving: timing; setting; selection of tapes; areas for discussion; relationship between individual sessions and overall aims; status of such sessions within the course overall; possibility of including one or two lectures early on in the Prelim. Programme.

I recommend that the school set up a working-party to consider the implications of this document for next year's Prelim. Programme. Such a working-party should consist of sector representations; one or two faculty who took part in this year's project; some of the students who took part in this year's project.

It might be good if we applied to TUT for funds so that we could video-tape some seminars of work in our School with a view to using these in any future Prelim. training programme.

REFERENCES

ABERCROMBIE, M.L.J. (1974) *Aims and Techniques of Group Teaching* (3rd edition) London Society for Research into Higher Education

BRADBURY, M. *The History Man* (1975) London Secker & Warburg

BRAMELD, T. (1955) 'Ethics of leadership' *Adult Leadership* 4 5-8

BRIDGES, D. (1975) 'The silent student' *Education for Teaching* 97 Summer 59-66

BRITISH COLUMBIA TEACHERS' FEDERATION (1970) *The Use of Discussion Groups for Exploration Purposes* (off-set litho pamphlet)

BRUNER,J.S. (1960) *The Process of Education* New York Vintage Books

CHAMBERS, P. (1973) 'Inter-collegiate cooperation in a scheme to use syndicate teaching methods with students following a course in the sociology of education' *Occasional papers in sociology and education* (mimeo) Association of Teachers in Colleges and Departments of Education

COLLIER, K.G. (1966) 'An experiment in university teaching' *Universities Quarterly* 20 Summer 336-347

COLLIER, K.G (1969) 'Syndicate methods: further evidence and comment' *Universities Quarterly* 23 Autumn 431-436

DUCKWORTH, R. (1970) 'The thinking behind the new course' in FLOOD PAGE, C. (ed) *Summary Report of a Symposium on Teaching Methods* (mimeo) 1-30 (symposium organised for staff and students of the Clinical Course of the Dental School of the London Hospital Medical College)

EPSTEIN, C. (1972) *Affective Subjects in the Classroom: Exploring Race, Sex, and Drugs* London Intext Educational Publishers

FAWCETT HILL, W. (1962) *Learning thru Discussion* London Sage Publications

GENN, J.M. (1972) 'Students' perceptions of secondary school teachers and university teachers – some specific major contrasts' *The Australian Journal of Education* 16 (1) 81-91

THE GREAT BOOKS DISCUSSION PROGRAM (1965) *A Manual for Co-*

Leaders 1 Chicago The Great Books Foundation

GROUP FOR RESEARCH AND INNOVATION IN HIGHER EDUCATION (1976) *Small Group Teaching: Selected Papers* The Nuffield Foundation

HOMERTON COLLEGE OF EDUCATION (1974) *Pilot Project on Small Group Teaching* (88 page duplicated report, compiled and edited by David Bridges)

THE HUMANITIES CURRICULUM PROJECT (1970) *The Humanities Curriculum Project: an Introduction* London Heinemann Educational Books Ltd

LAWRENCE, G. (1972) 'The syndicate method' *Varieties of Group Discussion in University Teaching* London University Teaching Methods Unit

MASON, C. (1971) quoted in TAYLOR, L.C. *Resources for Learning* Harmondsworth Penguin

MILES, M.B. (1959) *Learning to Work in Groups* Teachers' College Press, Columbia University

NISBET, S. (1966) 'A method for advanced seminars' *Universities Quarterly* 20 Summer 349-55

POWELL, J.P. (1974) 'Small group teaching methods in higher education' *Educational Research* 16 (3) 163-71

POWELL, J.P. and JACKSON, P. (1964) 'A note on a simplified technique for recording group interaction' *Human Relations* 17 289-91

REE, H. (1975) 'Between school and college' *The Daily Telegraph* 4 August

ROSENTHAL, R. and JACKSON, L. (1968) *Pygmalion in the Classroom* New York Holt, Rinehart and Winston

RUDDUCK, J. (1976) *Teaching Symmetry Theory in Seminars: a Study of an Innovation* Centre for Applied Research in Education, University of East Anglia

SCHEFFLER, I. (1955) *Conditions of Knowledge* Scott Foresman & Co

SMALL GROUP TEACHING PROJECT: Various documents and edited videotapes available from Jean Rudduck at the Centre for Applied Research in Education, University of East Anglia

STENHOUSE, L.A. (1972) 'Teaching through small group discussion: formality, rules and authority' *Cambridge Journal of Education* 2 (1) 18-24

UNIVERSITY GRANTS COMMITTEE (1964) *Report of the Committee on University Teaching Methods* (the Hale Committee) London HMSO

INDEX

DO NOT REMOVE
SLIP FROM POCKET